Enterprise Systems Architecture

Aligning Business Operating Models to Technology Landscapes

Daljit Roy Banger

Apress®

Enterprise Systems Architecture: Aligning Business Operating Models to Technology Landscapes

Daljit Roy Banger
London, UK

ISBN-13 (pbk): 978-1-4842-8645-6
https://doi.org/10.1007/978-1-4842-8646-3

ISBN-13 (electronic): 978-1-4842-8646-3

Managing Director, Apress Media LLC: Welmoed Spahr
Acquisitions Editor: Aditee Mirashi
Development Editor: James Markham
Coordinating Editor: Aditee Mirashi
Copy Editor: Kim Wimpsett

Cover designed by eStudioCalamar

Cover image designed by Freepik (www.freepik.com)

Distributed to the book trade worldwide by Springer Science+Business Media New York, 1 New York Plaza, Suite 4600, New York, NY 10004-1562, USA. Phone 1-800-SPRINGER, fax (201) 348-4505, e-mail orders-ny@springer-sbm.com, or visit www.springeronline.com. Apress Media, LLC is a California LLC and the sole member (owner) is Springer Science + Business Media Finance Inc (SSBM Finance Inc). SSBM Finance Inc is a **Delaware** corporation.

For information on translations, please e-mail booktranslations@springernature.com; for reprint, paperback, or audio rights, please e-mail bookpermissions@springernature.com.

Apress titles may be purchased in bulk for academic, corporate, or promotional use. eBook versions and licenses are also available for most titles. For more information, reference our Print and eBook Bulk Sales web page at http://www.apress.com/bulk-sales.

Printed on acid-free paper

A ruler must guard against two kinds of danger: one internal, coming from his own people; the other external, coming from foreign powers.

—Niccolò Machiavelli

Table of Contents

TABLE OF CONTENTS

About the Author

 **Daljit Banger** has 38 years of IT industry experience, having undertaken assignments in locations across the globe, including the United Kingdom, the United States, Sweden, Switzerland, Finland, Hong Kong, and Brazil, to name a few, on behalf of large, multinational companies.

Daljit has successfully managed several large professional teams of architects, has contributed to several publications, and is the author of several freeware software products for enterprise architecture.

Daljit holds a master of science (MSc) degree, is a Chartered IT Fellow of the British Computer Society (BCS), and chairs the BCS Enterprise Architecture Specialist Group.

About the Technical Reviewer

Tom Graves has been an independent consultant for more than four decades, in business transformation, enterprise architecture, and knowledge management. His clients in Europe, Australasia, and the Americas cover a broad range of industries including small-business, banking, utilities, manufacturing, logistics, engineering, media, telecoms, research, defense, and government. He has a special interest in whole-enterprise architectures for nonprofit, social, government, and commercial enterprises.

Acknowledgments

I want to thank the many people who provided valuable feedback, helpful comments, and ideas, especially the request to introduce a section on architectural impact assessments.

I would also like to thank the various reviewers especially Chris Banks, Tom Graves, and Dr. Colin Smart.

Preface

Over the past few decades, we have seen major transformations in the provision and consumption of technology services found in corporate landscapes and the supporting information ecosystems. These transformations have been driven by one, if not all, of the following factors:

- The *intelligent digital consumer*: This includes consumers who have an online presence, are armchair shoppers, are digitally informed, and can procure goods and services at the touch of a keystroke from a variety of geographically dispersed suppliers.

- *The value-driven lean organization*: This is a company operating in a competitive environment, with the drive to reduce operating expenses and time to market for its product.

- *New ways of working and service consumption*: This results from an anytime, anyplace, anywhere paradigm.

- *The pandemic*: Recently the pandemic has driven many organizations to introduce new contingency channels, operating models, and tools for collaboration, as well as location-independent productivity tools to support a workforce that had restrictions on movement.

- *Widespread digital presence*: A digital presence at various business touch points is needed to effectively interact with consumer demands, i.e., the provision of real-time, 24/7 system services to support the new business operating models.

- *Dispersed systems*: Distributed, federated, geographically dispersed systems are now required, as well as the subsequent "follow the sun" support models.

- *Dynamic environmental changes*: There is a need to innovate new business capabilities to meet dynamic environmental changes in consumption and trends.

- *Consumer devices*: Companies must support intelligent consumer devices, which connect and push information (diagnostic/intelligence) that transforms insights into consumption.

- *Open APIs*: Industries and organizations want to publish, expose, and federate system capabilities by creating an open API ecosystem.

- *Reduced time to market*: There is a need for reduced time to market for new systems, resulting in adoption of agile and new responsive system-design practices.

The previous drivers are just some of the considerations that have contributed to a rise in system complexity; although this is manageable for smaller organizations, it is not always the case for larger, multinational organizations with several hundreds of applications to support. This presents a daunting challenge for organizations in the form of control, support, management, and provision of systems.

Systems thinking, i.e., the overall approach for the analysis of a system's parts and how these components correlate and interact, over time, within the context of larger enterprise systems, has helped evolve general architecture thinking, i.e., the art and science of designing and building information systems, and has helped address, in part, some of the complexities that have arisen.

In today's digitally linked world, it would be exceedingly difficult for any dynamic organization to survive without a minimum set of technology capabilities driving delivery. These technology enablers become more complex in terms of volume, design, procurement, support, and management as organizations grow and thus require specialist architectural functions to control, design, manage, and deliver these capabilities in a secure/cost-effective way.

Specialist functions, such as enterprise architecture (EA), have evolved as a direct response to managing the complexity of systems. After all, these formal functions did not exist some 40 years ago when monolithic systems existed and were designed to handle tightly coupled multiple related functions.

The EA objective is to ensure technology landscapes and information ecosystems are optimized and aligned to meet operational goals and deliver capabilities that meet the strategic and tactical business needs for today and tomorrow.

Enterprise architecture, as a *function*, is primarily driven by the desire to invest and plan for technology through an economic lens, one in which both the macro and micro perspective viewpoints are factored into the design and any investment in technology by the organization.

Enterprise architecture, as a *discipline*, seeks to provide a line of sight in which the goal is to deliver high-value efficient systems that leverage reusable components, manage technology debt, and ensure information assets are managed and optimized as well as efficiently delivered for the enterprise.

Architecture, as an organizational *function*, especially the solution, information, and enterprise domains, has been triggered by a move from theoretical academic practices to front-line activities that now support functions such as strategic planning, budgeting, and delivering business and technology capabilities used to enable the new digital transformation agendas.

To support this evolution, a wide variety of architectural frameworks and styles have emerged during these decades with a common goal of delivering an enterprise architecture "service"; unfortunately, there is little commercial evidence or case studies demonstrating a *quantifiable* consistent return on investment, efficiency, and cost savings. However, attempts such as David F. Rico frameworks for measuring the ROI of EA [1] have provided a shift in the right direction.

This is primarily due to the use of a mix-and-match approach based on nonstandard approaches and in some cases over-complexity in delivery. However, the continuous improvement and maturity in small steps from within the architectural community has seen enterprise architecture as a discipline progress slowly and, more importantly, the associated mindset of architects has evolved.

Understanding technology, while important, should not be a key driver for developing enterprise architecture skills, especially as technology evolves and changes rapidly over time. Hence, the goal of the enterprise architect is to, irrespective of the technology enablers used to execute and deliver technology capabilities, have a macro view of the technology capabilities and the value it adds to the organization and the possible debt it could create if not managed.

The purpose of this book is share experience gained over several decades in the field, lay out a set of tools to help develop the enterprise and solution architecture mindset, and more importantly allow existing architects to refine their tools.

Before proceeding, it would be prudent to define some core terms that are used throughout this book; for additional terms, see the glossary. The following terms often get used in mixed contexts and are worthy of a mention:

Enterprise	Represents an Organisation or undertaking (*either commercial or non-profit*) that exists to deliver a specific set of products, services or capabilities to a set of consumers and can be represented by one or many *people, places and or things*.
Systems	A set of **things working together**, orchestrated to form a whole part of a mechanism or an interconnecting network which is encapsulated by Workflows, *Methods, Procedures and Routines* created to carry out a specific activity, duty, or to solve a single or multiple set of problems.
Architecture	Commonly referred to as the **art of *designing*** and ***building*** Systems and Structures which we adopt, adapt and extend to building Information Systems.
Capability	A generic term used to represent an ability to perform a set of core functions and or a set of specified task to deliver a targeted outcome.
Service	Provides an ability to deliver or do something of **material value**, often aggregated to provide a capability e.g. the business capability of Human Capital Management (HCM) which encapsulates several domains around people management.
Value	A benefit of sort, not limited to a monetary amount, where a value stream explored at the enterprise level allows for efficiency gains to be represented and optimised.
Governance	The action of controlling and managing a set of technology capabilities and the associated cost/expenditure, for an enterprise, together with the management of the associated risks.

Throughout this book, we will be interchangeably using the terms EA and ESA; however, the focus throughout will be on the systems and technology elements that are provided and aligned to support the business operating model (discussed throughout this book). Thus, our initial definition of EA is as follows:

> Enterprise architecture is not a method, principle, or doctrine. It is a way of thinking, a mindset, enabled by patterns, principles, frameworks, standards, etc., essentially seeking to align the technology ecosystem with the business operating model, i.e., with a trajectory driven by both the internal and external forces.

Absolute enterprise architecture should encapsulate areas relating specifically to the enterprise, i.e., the political, economic, social, and human factors that sit on the periphery of information systems design. This definition of the two disciplines can be summed up as follows:

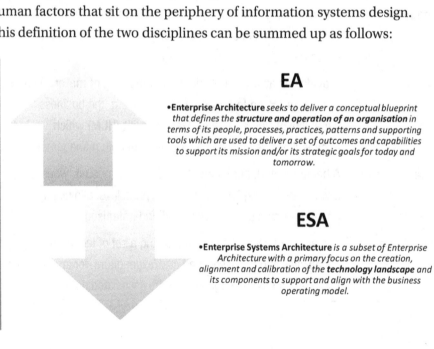

EA

- **Enterprise Architecture** *seeks to deliver a conceptual blueprint that defines the* **structure and operation of an organisation** *in terms of its people, processes, practices, patterns and supporting tools which are used to deliver a set of outcomes and capabilities to support its mission and/or its strategic goals for today and tomorrow.*

ESA

- **Enterprise Systems Architecture** *is a subset of Enterprise Architecture with a primary focus on the creation, alignment and calibration of the* **technology landscape** *and its components to support and align with the business operating model.*

The conceptual discipline of enterprise architecture covers the methods, tools, and techniques used to re-architect an organization to achieve its overall mission, goals, and objectives by including the restructuring of people, process, and technology with consideration given to the internal and external forces that impact the enterprise.

Enterprise architecture can cover a wide set of domains from the behavioral, sociopolitical elements to the technology components that achieve the redesign of the enterprise, and it is that wide lens that impacts the delivery of system capabilities.

We address the enterprise systems architecture viewpoint through Parts 1 through 4 and end with a focus on a key deliverable of an EA function in Part 5, i.e., developing an ICT strategy. Each part can be seen as a module for an undergraduate or postgraduate course and can be read and used independently of the other sections.

It must be stressed that we simply touch the surface of the various topics; especially in Parts 1, 3, and 4, readers are encouraged to "deep dive" further into the topics, but when they are all consolidated, they can provide a solid view of EA and the value it promotes.

When implemented, EA can act as a central support function across the enterprise and requires investment to enable delivery of a control and management mechanism to drive value for technology selection, introduction, and management across the organization.

Throughout we "touch" on topics to promote a way of thinking, i.e., an EA mindset, in Part 2 we introduce a taxonomy control framework, i.e., the *stack*, where we demonstrate the link between technology choices and business needs. This thus provides a mapping (audit) tool to provide the traceability for technology enablers to business capabilities.

The book is divided into five short parts; Part 2 is longer as it covers the stack, a core element. However, each section represents a self-contained unit and can be read individually. The appendix will present simple examples, acronyms, and other useful material.

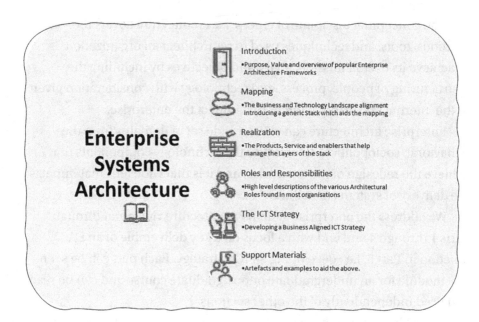

The products and roles discussed in Parts 3 and 4 present some "meat on the bone" and are provided to enable a better understanding of the deliverables, with Part 5 bringing it all together and highlighting a generic approach to developing an ICT strategy.

It would be prudent to highlight that within this book, we are *not* advocating a new EA method or playbook or promoting a specific framework. Our aim, as previously stated, is to develop the architectural mindset by introducing a commonsense notional stack that can be used, extended, and applied to multiple industries to explain concepts used by architectural teams to structure both thinking and work packages to deliver against the needs of the business.

Before you begin your journey through this book, it is important to note that enterprise architecture has emerged as a strange discipline, not because one is made to sit down and memorize a string of facts or rules to deliver the capabilities, but where the "thinking" evolves and develops as you move through the journey of discovery by working on real projects that help you understand it and that improves your sense of how the enterprise ecosystem coexists without placing too great an emphasis on the minutiae.

Who Should Read This Book?

This book is a valuable introduction for students and a guide for practitioners (including enterprise architects, IT architects, and solution, domain, business architects), business stakeholders (CTO, CIO, CEO), and others who work and provision systems capabilities to or for their organization.

The book aims to help develop the mindset of architects working at the enterprise and solution levels, while adding value to others who are interested in a generic approach to developing an IT strategy in business and elsewhere.

Some topics are just too broad to be covered in great depth but deserve a mention, and we recommend following the links provided for further information.

Introduction

The past few decades have been an exciting time for those of us working in the IT industry, witnessing a major disruption in the production and consumption of IT services. The fast-paced evolution has resulted in a spread of technology into every walk of life with most digital service consumers permanently plugged in and connected to vast information sources and services provided via the World Wide Web.

Changes have been rapid and innovative. These include changes such as the following:

- The increased application functionality, exceeding Moore's original law,[1] available to both organizations and consumers

- The rise of the digitally intelligent consumer

- The move from large monolithic, centralized, mainframe computers to a more geographically distributed, decentralized federated set of systems

- Widespread use of powerful end-user devices with more processing power than the early large computers of the 1970s

---

[1] Gordon Moore, the cofounder of Fairchild Semiconductor and Intel, saw that the number of transistors in a dense integrated circuit doubled about every two years. In his 1965 paper he described a doubling every year in the number of components per integrated circuit and projected this rate of growth would continue for at least another decade. In 1975, looking forward to the next decade, he revised the forecast to doubling every two years. This observation is referred to as Moore's law.

- The shift in data center hosting models resulting in a move to the "as a service"[2] model

- New and more mature technology supply models, outsourcing, and reallocation (onshore, offshore, nearshore)

- The growth of the Internet of Things (IoT), meaning consumer-connected devices

- The move to exposing information and systems capabilities through open API ecosystems

- New business models

This period of change for most businesses is driven by commercial globalization and the need for shorter time frames to get products and services to market supported by a drive to develop lean organizations with new working practices and cost models enabling the delivery of dynamic business system services.

Technology, without question, has been a key business catalyst at the heart of today's social and digital world, a world in which the 24/7 business operations adopt a follow-the-sun business model, requiring organizations to reshape and extend core business services and streamline process journeys, e.g., order to cash (O2C), to ensure distribution can support the anytime, anyplace, and anywhere business models to deliver the critical value.

In this modern digital world, in which there is an onus on interconnectivity, organizations have been forced to adapt and adopt new operating procedures, processes, and technology capabilities and modify general services as a response to the impact on operational environment

---

[2] Application as a service (AaaS), infrastructure as a service (IaaS), platform as a service (PaaS), and software as a service (SaaS) are all capabilities that can be delivered by a single or multiple vendors.

where agility, reliability, and robustness are key to execution as a cost-effective response.

The increased use of pervasive gadgets[3] e.g., mobile phones and tablets has boosted the demand for new organisational 'front door' digital services. These sevices demand access to complex back-end, real-time, "secure" processing systems. Historically these sevices were never exposed to consumers either directly or via system proxies and is best highlighted in financial sector with the increase of mobile banking.

This highlights the rise in complexity in terms of management and provision of IT systems and higher demands by users for new, innovative, interconnected systems and services where planning and provisioning for such systems is no mean feat, requiring IT departments (however branded[4]) to respond rapidly with technology capabilities that support new strategic and tactical needs.

The development of new systems is often riddled with risks, delays, and possible budget over-runs and ongoing support costs. Such risks have pushed organizations to adopt a "buy not build" route, i.e., procure and implement common off-the-shelf systems (COTSs) or services. This commodity-type approach to systems has resulted in a perception that IT is no longer a means to gaining a competitive advantage previously promoted in the theory of "first-mover advantages" by Porter,[5] but now more as a commodity business enabler.

One of the greatest challenges faced by many organizations is that short-term, tactical, low-cost commodity systems, perceived as delivering immediate benefits, often require additional capacity (hardware/network bandwidth), which can result in organizations accumulating technology debt (discussed later). Technology debt can arise in several ways that are

---

[3] Smart phones, tablets, Internet of Things (IoT) devices, digital watches, etc.

[4] Often IT departments, i.e., the departments that support and deliver the technology capabilities and services to the organization, are referred to as *corporate information systems, information systems group, group IT,* etc.

[5] Michael E. Porter, *Competitive Advantage.* See Part 5.

not envisaged when the system was originally commissioned, e.g., hosting model cloud adoption, software management, integration, etc.

A COTS solution providing services such as financial, human capital management (HCM), or enterprise resource planning (ERP) capabilities to large expensive systems will deliver on the Pareto principle[6] to fulfil the organization's needs, allowing organizations to modify their operations to "fit the package." However, these enterprise solutions tie the organization to the vendor's way of working and limit any competitive edge between organizations; thus, often extended or bespoke customization will incur additional costs to meet the tactical organizational needs.

As with all tactical solutions, there are hidden costs that manifest over time as systems are often shoehorned into organizations to meet a point-in-time need; they require resources to enable further collaboration and information sharing. Integration between a COTS package and a legacy in-house developed system is often difficult and as requirements change results in inevitable additional cost.

This building-block approach to acquiring systems is common among many large organizations, where the proliferation of smaller systems meeting the needs of small groups or individual users are procured and integrated into the organization where possible. The result of this proliferation is the creation of system silos or shadow IT systems that may not benefit the organization or enterprise as a whole.

We have described many issues faced by organizations, such as system proliferation, bespoke customization, integration, technology debt, etc., so how is this all managed or controlled? The answer in part is through the adoption of a unified, reusable, structured approach to managing technology landscape across the organization as promoted by enterprise architecture (EA). EA is sold as allowing organizations to plan, manage,

---

[6] The Pareto principle, also known as the 80/20 rule, states that, for many events, roughly 80 percent of the effects come from 20 percent of the causes. See Koch, Richard (1998).

and understand the characteristics of the enterprise in relation to the IT services that meet business needs.

Architecture is commonly defined as the process of designing buildings and infrastructures, which in a systems context we can expand to define as the art and science of constructing and designing information systems, technology capabilities, and services for the enterprise.

The term *enterprise systems architecture* (ESA) intentionally introduces an ICT bias to the role of the EA and simply extends the role to encapsulate the provision for strategic direction of IT capabilities in the organization and the supporting mechanisms of control to ensure that the technology landscape and business operating models are aligned.

Both terms are interchangeable. We will use EA to represent ESA throughout this book with a focus on technology to business alignment.

Depending on who you talk to, enterprise systems architecture can have several definitions, but for the purpose of clarity we will define it as follows:

> Enterprise systems architecture (ESA) can be viewed as the consolidation of years of systems thinking into a single domain, which seeks to align the organizational business activities, drivers, and needs with the relevant appropriate technology capabilities.

> These business drivers encapsulate the mission, goals, and objectives of the enterprise for both the present and future to drive the goal of ESA as one in which we leverage synergies across all systems platforms, ensuring that value is realized and added to minimizing technology debt, disruption, and silos.

The previous definition can be further classified as "the associated principles, policies, processes, patterns, and practices for aligning current and future business operating models, business processes and business information needs of the enterprise with the technology capabilities, enablers, and facilitators."

EA seeks to ensure that the ongoing strategic and tactical goals of the organization and associated business processes are supported by the appropriate and optimized applications, data models, technologies, and foundation technology services, which we will discuss as we move through the stack in the first part of this book.

So as an art, EA can be said to seek to align business needs, activities, and drivers with cost-effective technology capabilities for both today and tomorrow. The function of enterprise systems architecture, at a minimum and as illustrated in Part 3, seeks to do the following:

- *Control and govern* the introduction of new and existing technology capabilities and services into the organization and onto the technology estate

- *Inform* the business and relevant stakeholders on how to meet both strategic and tactical goals, while ensuring technical opportunities for cost reductions and efficiency gains are promoted; i.e., *advise* on the relevant levers that can be used to ensure the business outcomes are achieved

- *Direct* and promote through engagement with programs and projects of the use of technology to add value to the organization and ensure alignment and governance of the technology estate

Before proceeding to Part 1, it would be prudent to highlight that the approach adopted by many organizations to deliver the benefits of EA vary greatly, which has in and of itself presented problems trying to unify the standard products of EA, especially when each product has a hidden cost associated with production. Therefore, our goal in this book is to present a simple approach and provide some examples with the ultimate aim to help develop the EA mindset.

Where possible I have introduced several diagrams to highlight key concepts, as often an illustration conveys a stronger message than the associated words. To quote the famous advertising executive Fred R. Barnard, "One picture is worth a thousand words."

Further Material

Please visit my blog for additional content and updates:
`https://dalbanger.blogspot.com/`.

Please note that to preserve commercial and personal confidentiality, the case studies and examples in this book have been adapted, combined, and in part fictionalized in a variety of contexts. They do not and are not intended to represent any specific individual or organization, and the URLs for all document sources are in the public domain.

Trademarks or registered trademarks are acknowledged as the intellectual property of the respective owners, and URLs are provided to source material when used.

Part 1

In this part, we touch on the purpose and value of Enterprise Architecture (EA). We follow this with an overview of some of the popular frameworks that are used in the EA community.

CHAPTER 1

Architectural Purpose

An economical question often asked by academics, stakeholders, and critics of an enterprise architecture function is "Why should we, as a commercial organization, invest time and resources in a function that cannot show value in monetary terms or is difficult to measure or quantify?" EA, as with most central services, has an opportunity cost associated with it, i.e., a cost of a foregone alternative, one in which resources are diverted away from potentially critical project IT activities.

To address the question, we need to first define enterprise architecture and highlight its value. Then we will illustrate some of the indirect benefits delivered by operating a leaner operation and driving efficiency gains and indirect value.

Enterprise Architecture thinking has historically focused on the business operations layer and the subsequent drive for excellence and efficiencies by leveraging the synergies between its operations and the underlying IT Systems.

Unfortunately, this focus with a bias towards delivering IT Systems and not IT Services, has resulted in a budgeting approach in which the focus has been on delivering IT capabilities and not business services i.e., a bottom-up approach (discussed later in part 4) to IT Planning.

In Figure 1-1, we show how business operations sit at the heart of EA thinking; this is illustrated further when examining the numerous frameworks on the market. A *service* is exposed to the business operations as a reusable service and encapsulates capabilities that are managed to deliver value. This symbiotic relationship between the business operating

© Daljit Roy Banger 2022
D. R. Banger, *Enterprise Systems Architecture*,
https://doi.org/10.1007/978-1-4842-8646-3_1

model and technology capabilities is an ongoing process designed to assist and establish capabilities that support that operational model.

As previously mentioned, EA and ESA are interchangeable terms, with ESA having an emphasis on systems, i.e., processes, practices, and patterns that align the technology landscape to the business operational models, allowing management to justify, budget, and plan for the successful realization of the benefits of technology.

As we have seen on many technology projects that have failed, despite the strategy being clearly articulated, performance is often attributed to either poor execution or lack of clarity or direction of the downstream technology services being deployed. Enterprise systems architecture seeks to add clarity in the form of the mapping, i.e., audit trail, justification, and alignment, to existing platforms to ensure that the benefits are realized.

In most organizations, the enterprise architecture function is delivered by a team within the information technology departments, and therefore the underlying duty of care for the team has to date been to provide technology capabilities. The purpose then of enterprise architecture, i.e., why it exists as a function, is to provide the support and guidance required to any project, system, or process that may impact the technology ecosystem of the organization to support its operations while addressing technology enablers for the business operational models.

Figure 1-1 highlights some of the demarcation points in EA thinking, where the classic view to date has been IT-centric, having stemmed from the IT function. ESA is our extension of that original thinking, with the focus on aligning the technology capabilities not with the requirements but with the business operating models and the technology to service those needs. It should be noted that an additional layer of EA thinking has evolved to focus on the softer skills with a sociological and psychological bias, which is not in scope for this book.

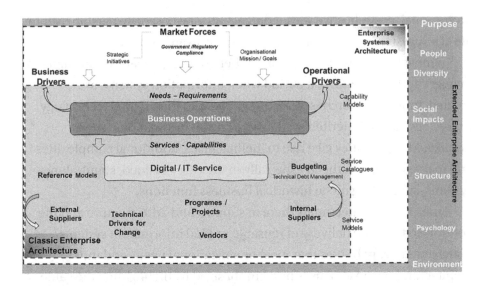

Figure 1-1. *Business operations, the focus of ESA*

Figure 1-1 also explains how any definition of EA may vary between members of the architecture community, subject to the lens through which they view the topic, i.e., the business or systems-centric viewpoints.

Technology is now perceived as a critical enabler for many organizations and a shift in organizational priorities with the appetite for both risk and technical disruption are exhibited by the increase in level of IT spend as a proportion of organizational budgets. This statistic was highlighted in the 2018 Deloitte [2] U.S. Insight Report which reported that the overall average for all industries of the allocated IT Budgets was 3.28 % of revenue and even higher with Banking and Securities at 7.16%. In large organizations these percentages represent are significant figure and require management, a primary goal of the EA.

The control and direction provided by EAs for managing the technology ecosystem aims to drive efficiency savings especially when the cost of providing IT services represents a significant part of annual budgets. So, EA must ensure that all processes in delivering services and IT capabilities are optimized, meet current needs, and are delivered in a controlled, professional, cost-effective way, reducing the total cost of ownership over the life of any system in terms of applications, hardware, support, etc.

In most instances organizations either grow organically or through mergers and acquisitions, a period when information systems are created, inherited, purchased, or integrated into the existing technology ecosystem. These inherited systems, can result in situations where duplicated capabilities give rise to inefficiencies, additional complexities and management overhead especially in the case of siloed, stand-alone systems, supporting niche historical business functions.

Enterprise architecture is there to support and add structure and the controls to facilitate delivery of reusable unified information systems/ management capabilities that meet organizational needs and thus architectural purpose. This is best emphasized by highlighting the value derived in terms of the following:

- *Reuse* of technology components, processes, and other artifacts to provide reduced support costs across divisions, e.g., the adoption of common tools, using a single interface to support common repeatable processes

- *Extension* of existing capabilities, like reuse, but with the emphasis of extending existing systems with minor changes

- *Simplification* of the technology used and introduced into the estate, eliminating any cost associated with duplication

- *Standardization* on single platforms and the use of common technology enablers to ensure that any new components complying with the standard can be easily introduced, managed, and supported at the lowest unit cost across the organization

- *Services-level improvement* achieved through understanding common systems problems and any bottlenecks by analyzing patterns of usage and incidents that arise during use and establishing a "quick fix" remediation program

- *Remediation* of technology bottlenecks that are impacting the business and any related technical debt across the organizational boundaries (internal/external) to ensure that this is best minimized over time

We discussed briefly the why, i.e., the importance of EA as a discipline, which we will expand on further with our discussion of the three core functions of controlling, informing, and directing technology investment and management decisions. However, before we proceed to the what, it would be prudent to briefly mention some of architectural approaches and styles found in many popular frameworks.

Architectural Approaches/Styles

Over the past few decades, we have seen enterprise architecture undergo incremental development and changes, championed by various frameworks each with a different approach and style for delivery.

To meet industry-specific requirements, e.g., the need for compliance in banking or the need for quality controls in manufacturing, we have seen variations in frameworks and the resulting artifacts, which have a bias and prioritization toward the industry they serve.

However, core EA principles have remained the same, i.e., the provision of a framework to support a unified standard approach for managing and delivering technology capabilities to meet the specific desired business outcomes.

Industries and vendors have collaborated to define reference architectures or frameworks that help align and modularize business and technology assets in a predictable way. These repeatable architectures allow organizations to differentiate products and services and reuse commodity resources where efficiencies can be gained.

Frameworks try to present a generic "one size fits all" set of reusable patterns to deliver an EA capability. However, like most patterns, they leave the user to mix and match attributes; i.e., they do not often present the details required and simply refer you to other sources and variations in the artifacts. These variants pose a major challenge for organizations on the journey of adopting a single approach to delivering architectural realization, as adoption requires investment in developing the structure and artifacts, which further assist with the governance/management of all IT systems.

As well as frameworks, there also exists a wide range of architectural styles, which present approaches to building information systems. This in a sense dilutes the EA debate and should not be confused with enterprise architecture frameworks. These styles are best highlighted using the terms *driven* and *oriented*. In this style of architecture, a specific focal area is adopted as a baseline to deliver an IT system to the organization. Some examples of such styles worthy of further study are as follows:

- *Domain-driven architecture*: This is very much about the construction of enterprise applications, where the focus is on a business or operational domain. It captures use cases, logic, and interactions for that domain, allowing an iterative build of the IT system. Use cases focus on a understanding around the specific problem or business function that is captured in the domain or its subdomains.

- *Business-driven architecture*: This is a top-down approach to developing information systems in which the business drives things, with stakeholder participation, and prioritizes the capabilities it wants. In other words, the business architecture is built as a set of IT portfolios (programs/projects) deploying capabilities and process automations through a set of regular transformations controlled by the business.

- *Model-driven architecture*: This is an approach in which a set of guidelines, specifications, or models are used to build information systems extending the domain approach.

- *Process-driven architecture*: This refers to design by problem solving, i.e., the use of a formal scalable process as a main approach to solving problems. It is executed by a team of problem solvers. As a formally defined methodology, it opens itself up to continuous improvement.

- *Event-driven architecture*: This is an architecture style that relates to the production, detection, consumption of, and reaction to business or technical events where an event is a change in state, or an update, e.g., where a current account balance moves to a negative amount and triggers a set of overdraft system actions.

- *Service-oriented architecture*: This adopts an approach where a set of services are exposed for consumption by the application components, through a communication protocol over a network remaining independent of any product, vendor, or technology. (See Thomas Erl for a detailed analysis.)

The above approaches are all worthy of a mention and further scrutiny. However, they all have a common bias i.e., the delivery of a IT System and in most cases ignore our core EA tenets, which is evolves around the ongoing alignment of these information systems and associated components to the business operating model for today and tomorrow.

Organizational adoption of any enterprise architectural style or framework must deliver greater control and efficiency for all IT operations, providing a structured/reusable approach to management, creation, and adoption of enterprise-wide technology.

In many cases, adopting an enterprise framework, meta-model, or architectural style by an organization and going through the relative certification processes represents a big commitment, in terms of manpower, tool adoption, and license cost, all factors that must be considered when selecting a framework.

Architects adopt and oscillate between different architecture frameworks to utilize what best fits their organization, so no singular framework is ever fully used within any organization, but a mix of features or artifacts are adopted.

We will introduce a "lightweight" concept/approach to enterprise systems architecture by introducing a stack that focuses on the mindset of practitioners with no specific "cookbook." However, no book on enterprise architecture would be complete without a brief overview of popular frameworks. These popular frameworks have each contributed to the current direction of enterprise architecture, and each framework is well-documented elsewhere. Each one has significant strengths and weaknesses, as shown in Figure 1-2.

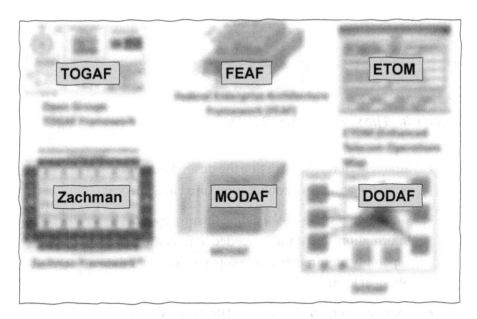

Figure 1-2. *The myriad of EA frameworks/taxonomies*

UK Ministry of Defence Architecture Framework

The Ministry of Defence Architecture Framework (MODAF) is an architecture framework that defines a standardized way of conducting enterprise architecture within a military context by providing a set of rules and templates, known as *views*. These views, when populated, provide a graphical and textual visualization of the business area being investigated.

It is important to note that, at the time of this writing, MODAF has been replaced with the NATO Architecture Framework (NAF) V4, details of which can be found at the NATO website [3]. However, the material available for MODAF is still publicly available and presents a great opportunity to explore the methodology.

MODAF views are divided into seven categories; each one offers a different perspective on the business area for stakeholder interests and promotes consistency between the views, as depicted in Figure 1-3.

Figure 1-3. *The seven views of MODAF*

- Strategic views (StVs) define the desired business outcome and the capabilities required to achieve it.

- Operational views (OVs) define the processes, information, and entities needed to fulfil the capability requirements in a conceptual rather than a physical form.

- Service-oriented views (SOVs) describe services required to support the processes described in the operational views.

- Systems views (SVs) describe the physical implementation of the operational and service-oriented views and thus define the solution.

- Acquisition views (AcVs) describe the dependencies, milestones, and timelines of the schemes that will deliver the solution.

- Technical views (TVs) define standards that are applied to the solution.

- All views (AVs) provide a description and glossary of the contents of the architecture.

Further information and examples on these views can be found on the UK government website [3].

U.S. Department of Defense Architecture Framework

U.S. Department of Defense Architecture Framework (DoDAF) is an architecture framework from the U.S. Department of Defense (DoD) and provides a visualization platform for military stakeholders and represents areas of interests through viewpoints organized by a set of views.

Models are described by the following viewpoints:

> The All Viewpoint describes the main aspects of architecture context that relate to all viewpoints; it's a kind of level 0 view.

> The Capability Viewpoint represents the capability needs, capability maps, and delivery timing.

> The Data and Information Viewpoint represents the data requirements, relationships, flows, and structures for delivering the capability and meeting any operational requirements.

> The Operational Viewpoint includes the operational scenarios, activities, and requirements that support and deliver the desired capabilities.

> The Project Viewpoint describes the relationships between the operational and capability requirements and the various programs or projects of work being implemented, and it details dependencies between capability and operational requirements within the framework of the defense acquisition system process, etc.

The Services Viewpoint is the design for solutions including the nonfunctional elements for performers, activities, services, and their exchanges to provide the operational and capability support functions.

The Standards Viewpoint captures the business, technical, operational and industry policies, standards, guidance, and constraints that will apply to the capability and operational requirements delivered.

The Systems Viewpoint presents multiple views relating to the design of the solution and documenting the systems, modules components, connectivity, and any context delivering for or supporting operational and capability functions.

The full details of the framework can be found on the U.S. DoD website [4].

The Open Groups TOGAF® Framework

TOGAF® is one of the most popular frameworks on the market; it has evolved since the mid-1990s, with a large community of volunteers developing the standard currently, at version 10.

The TOGAF® framework allows organizations to define repeatable processes for developing their EA. TOGAF® is well-documented and flexible in its usage, allowing organizations to customize it accordingly to meet their needs. As a process enabler, TOGAF® provides the Architecture Development Method (ADM) process, which prompts users to start at the vision phase (i.e., architectural scope, identification of stakeholders, and getting approvals) and follow the various processes so that users eventually get to the Architecture Change Management process.

TOGAF® provides several reusable artifacts for organizations to leverage, such as the following:

- ADM process

- Content framework

- Reference material

- Guidelines/techniques

- Capability models

TOGAF® and its extremely large community provide a comprehensive arsenal of tools, but at its heart it promotes four views (shown in Figure 1-4) of the architecture (business, application, data, and technical). These are initial deliverables in the ADM Architecture Vision phase and are enhanced through iterations.

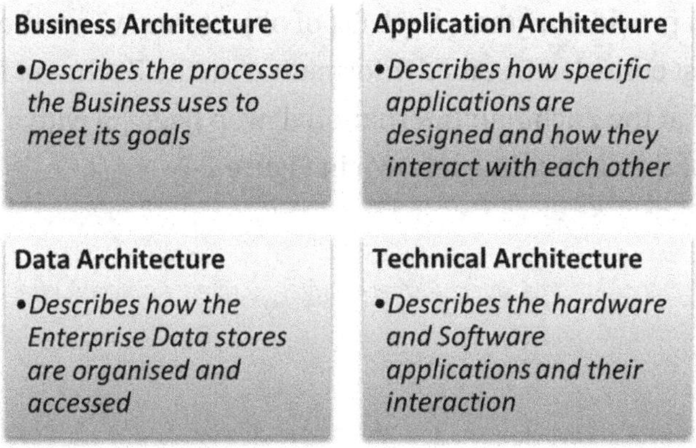

Business Architecture
- *Describes the processes the Business uses to meet its goals*

Application Architecture
- *Describes how specific applications are designed and how they interact with each other*

Data Architecture
- *Describes how the Enterprise Data stores are organised and accessed*

Technical Architecture
- *Describes the hardware and Software applications and their interaction*

Figure 1-4. *TOGAF's® four views*

TOGAF® provides a detailed set of products for its architectural process that requires extensive commitment by organizations, in terms of training, production of artifacts, and overall stakeholder buy-in.

Detailed information on TOGAF® can be found on the Open Group website, and version 10 (subject to registration) can be downloaded for free [5].

Zachman Framework

The Zachman Framework™ is not a methodology for creating the implementation (an instantiation) of the objects resulting in an enterprise ontology.

The framework has stood the test of time. It has been around for several decades and has added great value to the enterprise architectural debate. It is commonly used as a taxonomy, i.e., a check list, and although referred to as a framework, it is used for organizing architectural artifacts (in other words, design documents, specifications, and models) that consider both who the artifact targets (for example, the business owner and builder) and what particular issue (for example, data and functionality) is being addressed.

Zachman provides a great check list of objects and views the enterprise architect must consider. Detailed information on the Zachman framework can be found at the Zachman International® web page [6] with a complete description of the elements, as shown in Figure 1-5.

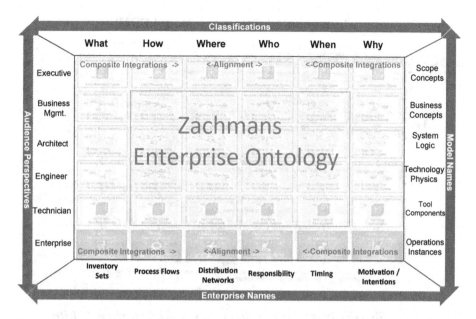

Figure 1-5. *The Zachman Framework for EA (source: Zachman.com)*

Federal Enterprise Architecture Framework

The U.S. Federal Enterprise Architecture Framework (FEAF) was established in 1999 by the chief information officers (CIOs). The purpose of the FEAF was to facilitate the shared development of common processes and information among U.S. federal agencies and other government agencies.

FEAF has a comprehensive taxonomy, like Zachman, and an architectural process like TOGAF®, which can be adapted for private enterprises. FEAF provides several tools, e.g., the the Consolidated Reference Model (Figure 1-6), allowing government departments and agencies to adopt a common language to describe and analyze investments.

Consolidated Reference Model CRM)

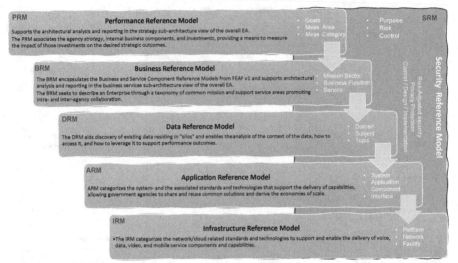

Figure 1-6. *FEAF: Consolidated Reference Model (source: White House Archives)*

FEAF allows a given architecture to be partitioned into business, data, applications, and technology architectures, where:

- The b*usiness* architecture represents the business functions that the organization performs and the information that the organization uses.

- The *data* architecture defines how data is stored, managed, and used in a system. It establishes common guidelines for data operations that make it possible to predict, model, and control the flow of data in the system.

- The *application* architecture consists of logical systems that manage the data objects in the data architecture and support the business functions in the business architecture. The applications are defined without reference to specific technologies.

- The *technology* architecture describes current and future technical infrastructure and specific hardware and software technologies that support organizational information systems. It provides guidance and principles for implementing technologies within the application architecture.

For additional information, see the U.S. government website for more information [7].

Meta-Models/Reference Architectures

Industries such as finance require formal agreements for data interchange to be agreed on up front between all parties in the community, e.g., SWIFT [8]. Such agreements and standards promote consistency and integrity of information exchange across the industry and between individual participants.

The building block for these standards is the agreement of a definition for core objects, e.g., identifiers such as Person, Address, or Product. These form a baseline model that is agreed on by all parties.

A meta-model is a *model of a model* that describes the basic elements that act as the foundation or baseline for an industry. When used by an individual organization, it can build a foundation that can be tailored for the organization, which indirectly imposes standards across that industry.

Meta-models are powerful tools and are often artifacts developed by EA communities within the industry who understand the key facets that are integral to their industry and that produce a level macro (level 0) view.

Figure 1-7 illustrates how an organization in the industry that inherits a model can expand the base model (schematic/objects) creating a unified architectural approach across the industry.

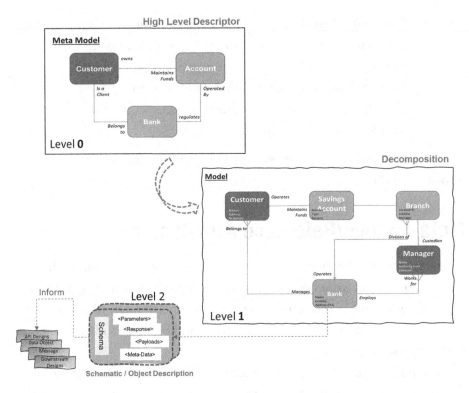

Figure 1-7. *Meta-models: the building block for standards*

The meta-model, at a very basic level, defines a common language for expressing a model and any sets of related models. The meta-models also seek to provide a framework within which the model can be constructed and can conceptualize any meta-types.

Developing and extending a meta-model is a time-consuming task and difficult to demonstrate the initial benefits to an audience. However, EAS adopts meta-modeling as a core deliverable of its service to conduct analysis, construction, and development of the frames, rules, constraints, and theories applicable to allow them to analyze complex problems within their organization.

A meta-model typically defines the languages and processes and a concept map illustrating all the main classes of concepts from which we can form a model serving as the explanation and definition of relationships among the various components of the applied model itself. The following are two good examples of an industry-specific meta-model:

- The ACORD [9] Reference Architecture provides an EA framework for the insurance industry.

- The MODAF meta-model (M3) is the reference model that underpins MODAF [10].

Summary

In this chapter, we introduced the various architectural styles, often labeled as a *driven* or *oriented* architecture. These styles are often well-documented and deliver both value and structure to architectural thinking.

We then proceeded to highlight some of the popular architectural frameworks. Frameworks result in industry "cookbooks" with basic shared recipes (patterns) that are often created in collaboration for the good of an industry.

By introducing the architectural styles and frameworks, we hope you concluded that they are similar in the desired outcome, i.e., to deliver a IT ecosystem that aligns to a specific individual or group of business needs.

To fully appreciate the EA frameworks and the commonality between them architectural, we encourage a deeper dive.

Part 2

In this part, we introduce a taxonomy approach (a stack) and show examples for each layer. This allows EAs to appreciate the areas that should be part of their overall mindset.

CHAPTER 2

The Stack

In this chapter, we revert to the basics and introduce a simple canvas, which we will refer to as the *stack*. We will deconstruct the components using examples to provide a greater understanding for the mindset of an EA.

Against this wireframe we introduce a "notional" architectural stack that can be sliced and diced to present a clearer understanding of the technology landscape and its alignment to the business operations models.

Systems and architectural frameworks evolve and develop over time, capturing and building on real-world experiences and adopting best practices along the way that provide input into our stack. This is complemented by input from several thought leaders referenced accordingly.

The stack aims to present a visualization that enables a control checklist for enterprise systems architecture (ESA). With the introduction of a simple "multilayered" set of building blocks, one can view and link an organization's business and technology, a simple notional mapping with current and future business needs considered.

The result of any changes in any business, both external and internal, requires a 360° view across the estate to ensure that the impact of any change is measured and assessed in terms of both the support for technology components and the associated processes required for business operations.

© Daljit Roy Banger 2022
D. R. Banger, *Enterprise Systems Architecture*,
https://doi.org/10.1007/978-1-4842-8646-3_2

The conceptual stack presented provides a simple layered framework, ensuring a comprehensive understanding of the elements required to factor in the multiple areas of the enterprise technology and supported by reusable patterns and tools. The stack as a resource highlights and leverages many tools that are presented as learning aids only.

The Architectural Stack

One can view and represent an enterprise and its architecture in many ways, e.g., as a set of canvas sheets with multiple views, a network of functional domains, etc. However, the views we adopt and expand are a set of horizontal layers, each inter-linked in both directions and spanning the internal and external elements of an organization. These internal and external relationships support the ability to maintain and manage a 360° view of how technology is aligned, calibrated, and exposed to meet the requirements and needs of the organization.

These 360° views support an understanding of the dependencies, impacts, and interactions, enabling a view in which we can present how a change in one variable will have a ripple effect in other areas; e.g., a change in law using the stack can show the impacted areas (see the GDPR and Payment Industry/Open Banking API example in the appendix).

We refer to this layered view as the *stack*; it has several components, as depicted in Figure 2-1, and a set of interrelated domains that all collaborate to support the business operating model (BOM). It must be stressed that each component represents quite a large domain and in absolute terms could warrant its own book. At its heart the architectural stack represents an abstract visual of the interaction between key business areas of concern and the technology landscape of the organization at a given point in time.

One of the many benefits of presenting a set of independent domains as in Figure 2-1 is the ability to reflect the effect of a change by highlighting both the upstream and downstream process impacts, e.g., the introduction of a new legislation that affects the enterprise.

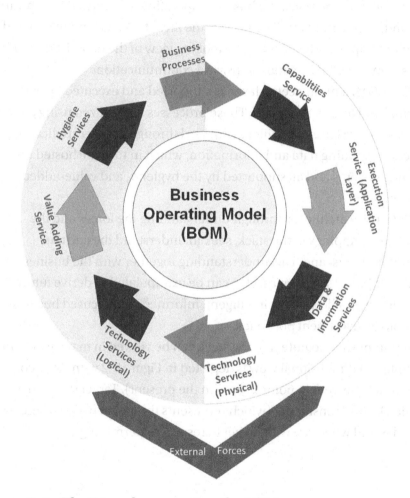

Figure 2-1. *The EA cycle supporting the BOM*

Understanding the domains in the stack allows systems professionals to take a "divide and conquer" approach to plan for new capabilities and mitigate any future organizational risk from the modification of the technology landscape, e.g., changes to existing systems, upgrades, and introduction of new systems or processes changes that require a new use of existing technology, etc.

We will dissect each domain of the stack, but it is important to note that the heart of the stack, the business operating model (BOM), can vary from industry to industry. The BOM is the layer that has both the inward and more importantly the outward-looking view of the organization in terms of interactions, relationships, and communications.

The BOM, a multifaceted layer, is supported and executed by both informal and formal processes. These processes are realized using generic services and systems capabilities provided through various applications and corresponding data and information, which in turn are hosted on enabling systems and all supported by the hygiene- and value-added services.

Enterprise architects, through understanding the forces and the associated mappings in the stack, seek to understand the current technology landscape. This understanding together with the business drivers, objectives, strategies, etc., can be extrapolated to derive future possible states, allowing for intelligent, informed, and focused business technology investment portfolios.

It is important to note that the stack can be viewed in many ways; an example of a dimensional view is depicted in Figure 2-2 with three core timeframes: Current (a point in time in the present), Target (the end goal position), and Transitional (which represents the gap between where we are today and where we want to get to resources permitting).

Although Current and Target have fixed "time points," Transitional may well have multiple representations that are spread over numerous timeframes, i.e., have multiple views associated with the state changes, e.g., year 1, year 2, etc.

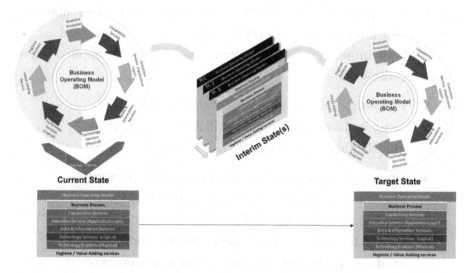

Figure 2-2. *Current, Transitional, and Target states*

The layers, as shown in the interim states, are ordered to present a logical stack for most organizations. These layers can be re-organized to closely align to the needs of the business. For example, capabilities and business processes can be rotated to represent business processes sitting below capabilities or capabilities and services. Our goal is to highlight the layers and the interactions, but feel free to modify them to meet your organizational needs.

The domains interact both horizontally and vertically. A component in one layer can consume and produce services for the layer above and below. These layers are briefly described in the following sections.

Layers Expanded and Explored

Each layer in the stack should be considered a self-contained entity with components that have individual characteristics, execution properties, or rules that are unique to that layer. When decomposed, these components can trigger, push, or consume a service or outcome from the layer above or below; i.e., the flow/exchanges between each layer are bidirectional.

With this in mind, the following are the rules that can be applied when considering the stack:

- Every organization, irrelevant of size, be it a commercial or not-for-profit, will have an operating model either created, adopted, or inherited.

- Organizations will seek to optimize or restructure their operating model to deliver maximum value to their organizations through optimization and efficiency savings to deliver critical value to internal and external stakeholders regularly, especially in times of environmental turbulence; in other words, operational conditions change.

- Operating models are supported by both formal and informal processes.

- Processes are delivered through a group or single set of orchestrated services or capabilities.

- Capabilities can be rendered or presented via a single or group of application services.

- Applications exploit and leverage information and data services to deliver value to the capabilities.

- Capabilities and services are supported by technology enablers wrapped around sets of hygiene services (discussed later).

- Any changes in structure or delivery of a business operating model will impact the downstream components and may result in required changes in the technology ecosystem, i.e., have an impact either on technology or processes.

Figure 2-3 decomposes the stack and provides a "checklist" to be used for a better understanding of the components that appear in each layer of the stack. In some industries, these may or may not apply and can be further extended to meet the needs of the industry.

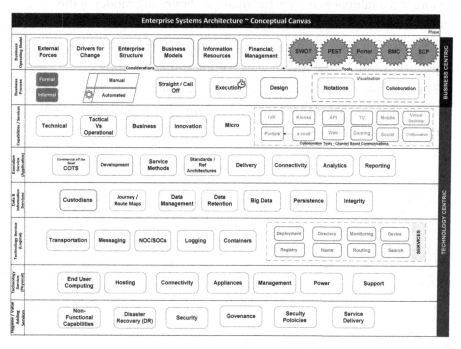

Figure 2-3. *The stack*

The stack is provided in the appendix with several examples, i.e., the next level of decomposition. The visualization benefits are immense, especially as a governance mechanism presenting a unified view of the variables for the EA by highlighting how making a change in one system component in any layer can have an impact on many other systems or processes and ultimately thus in the BOM.

Summary

In this chapter, we introduced the stack and subsequently introduced a group of independent yet interdependent layers that when aggregated present a view of the technology ecosystem and more importantly the support and enablers to realize the business operating model of the enterprise.

The introduction of the stack and the states (Current, Interim, and Target) bring a simplistic way to view complex organizations.

The example decomposition of the stack in Figure 2-3 can be used as a baseline for enterprise architects to build up their knowledge of their organization's technology ecosystem.

CHAPTER 3

Layer 0: The Business Operating Model

The business operating model (BOM) or layer 0 is the foundation for all business activities and thus considered the most important of all layers, encapsulating both the inward- and outward-facing elements of the organization, impacting all subsequent downstream activities.

Before discussing the BOM, we should highlight a common misconception and the clear differences between a BOM and a business model.

- A *business model* is focused on the way in which a company is structured to generate revenue, make a profit, or deliver its charter from both its internal and external operations. The business model represents the model of how an organization will structure itself or adapt to create, deliver, and realize value for its stakeholders considering both the internal/external boundaries and constraints.

- A *business operating model* is the whole operational aspect of the business to support the previous and more. As the name suggests, it is the modus operandi for the organization, i.e., its operational response to deliver the outcomes and capabilities required and to support the delivery of the business model.

© Daljit Roy Banger 2022
D. R. Banger, *Enterprise Systems Architecture*,
https://doi.org/10.1007/978-1-4842-8646-3_3

Irrespective of the type or size of the organization or even its funding, it can be argued that at a basic level all enterprises perform one of four activities (Figure 3-1). These distinct activities center around an organization ingesting something (person, object, or thing) into their operational structures and the outcome being performed, as one of the following activities, to deliver intrinsic value.

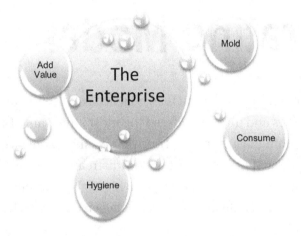

Figure 3-1. *Four functions found in all enterprises*

The functions are as follows:

1. Add value to that something or increment the perceived value to a consumer.

2. Mold the something to meet a specific specification or desired outcome that adds value.

3. Consume the something to enable it to operate or deliver value.

4. Perform a form of the hygiene function on the something, before pushing it out to its customers, clients, or third parties either publicly or privately to achieve its goals.

The previous has a common thread, i.e., one of "adding value or a perceived value" to a consumer.

So, it is important to use when considering our analysis of a BOM allowing one to further segment work packages to explore the flow of objects and the value derived during and at each stage of that flow.

Analysis of a BOM can range from the extremely complex, as one would expect for large multiregional and multinational corporations (MNCs), to the relatively simple for a small to medium enterprise. This complexity can directly map to the number of processes assigned to support the formal and informal techniques required. For the sake of illustration, as in Figure 3-2, we divide the BOM into two segments: the considerations and tools, and methods and frameworks.

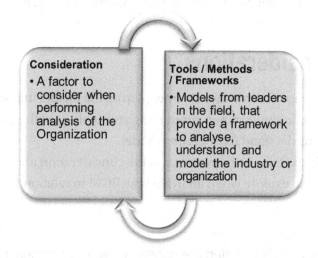

Figure 3-2. BOM analysis: considerations and tools

The business operating model layer is the enterprise, and all services below it exist to assist and support by providing services to enable its goals or outcomes. A change in any of the dynamics of the BOM will have an impact on the way it consumes and delivers any downstream supporting services.

A BOM can highlight the behavioral characteristics of an organization and subsequent influences in terms of the manner of operation found in its structures and interactions (internal and external) when trying to achieve its mission, goals, and objectives.

It is important that the CIO and the enterprise architects, at a minimum, understand and capture structures, interactions, and flows both internal and external to the organization to ensure adequate technology support is available to execute the organizational mission, goals, and objectives.

BOMs, when contextualized, provide insight into the domains of the business that require servicing for the enterprise to function and exist. Several common tools exist, which we will discuss briefly, that support the development or understanding of relevant business models in this layer.

BOM Considerations

We will now deep dive into layer 0, by exploring the factors that should be considered and included when conducting any analysis of the enterprise and trying to understand its operating model.

We briefly explain the importance of the consideration and some possible areas to explore when analyzing the BOM in relation to the EA lenses.

Note   Considerations listed are generic to most industries, and some considerations may have a greater weight than others in terms of importance for the enterprise.

Considerations encapsulate several areas. In Figure 3-3 we consolidate some of the key considerations that are further discussed in the following text.

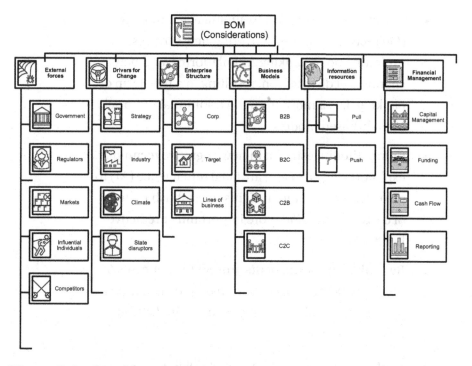

Figure 3-3. *Consideration map*

External Forces: Industry Shapers and Disruptors

All organizations are subject to external forces that impact, directly or indirectly, its operating model and can shape the industry moving forward.

External forces represent both events and entities that may impact your organization, over which you have zero or limited control. These require scanning to ensure that any impact or change can be managed, and risks are provisioned, for process and resources assigned to minimize the exposure to the organization with mitigations put in place as a defense.

We can assess the external environment, through examination of any industry, e.g., the global financial services industry (2020), where we observe trends that will ultimately change the dynamics of the industry, the organizational participation, and especially the technology capabilities required by participants to thrive. These trends are as follows:

- The emergence of the new financial technology (FinTech) companies delivering new services, exploiting open banking API platforms, and new channels of distribution, resulting in a new form of banking, i.e., a move from the traditional red-brick, branch-based models

- Competitor investment in new cognitive techniques exploiting Big Data and artificial intelligence (AI) to gain clearer customer insights to establish patterns of current usage and more importantly predictive behaviors

- Rethinking by participants around the concepts of money with the challenge from crypto currencies, tokens, stablecoins, and the blockchain distributed ledger technologies

- Increased spend by rivals around digital transformations to modify legacy back-end processes and front-end customer focused systems and new banking experiences

In the financial services industry, the previous shapers and industry disruptors will impact the current BOM of existing participants and more importantly their technology landscapes. These forces will reshape the industry moving forward.

As well as the pressure from trends in the industry, external forces also come from a multitude of other sources ranging from government legislations, competitor/consumer behaviors and actions, market forces, and even in some cases influential individuals who have a stake in the direction the organization is taking.

Questions one should ask when analyzing the BOM are

- What are the external forces at play in the industry?

- What, if any, is the impact on the enterprise from these external forces?

- Does this impact affect the current way the organization must or can conduct its activities?

These are simple questions to address, which when answered can impact the miscellaneous investment levers to be modified, mitigated for, or provisioned for meeting the BOM objectives.

Legal rules are external forces found across all industry sectors and subject to regulatory compliance,[1] which is often mandated as a rule to participate in that industry. For example, companies must adhere to information privacy acts when operating in specific jurisdictions. Some examples of privacy acts are listed here:

- United States Privacy Act (USA)

- Data Protection Act 2018/UK GDPR (UK)

- General Data Protection Regulation (Europe)

- Information Protection and Electronic Documents Act (Canada)

- Personal Data Protection Bill (India)

- Privacy Act 1988 (Australia)

While government and regulators are at the top of the list in terms of compliance, it must be noted that market forces should be analyzed to assess changes that can impact the organization, e.g., new entrants with innovative technology, lean processes, or a disruptive nature.

---

[1] Regulatory compliance is an organization's adherence to the domestic or international laws, regulations, guidelines, and specifications relevant to its industry. Violations of regulatory regulations can result in legal punishment including fines from the various authorities.

Figure 3-4. *External forces/industry shapers summary*

Drivers for Change

Drivers for change represent elements both internal and external to an organization that are nudging or "driving" an organization to adapt, adopt, or change its current practices and processes, resulting in a transformation to achieve a new desired state.

Organizations are dynamic, i.e., do not remain static. This is a state of flux in terms of its goals, operations, and structures especially when transactional volumes increase or decrease.

Industry shapers, as explained earlier, in times of turbulence or disruption, can have an impact on the operational system, especially when organizations opt to respond to these changes by adjusting or recalibrating its operations to meet the changes.

These drivers, which invoke a change, should be highlighted where possible and maybe weighted during any analysis to enable further impact analysis. The following are some examples of drivers for change:

- A change in organizational direction initiated by a new senior management team, with a new agenda and adjustment to the overall businesses strategy resulting in a change to the organization purpose or direction

- A social or behavioral change by customers or consumers of the products or services provided by the organization

- An environmental driver for change, i.e., becoming eco-friendly and sustainable or adopting a net zero policy

- A mandatory new piece of legislation that will come into force

- Industry disruptors, meaning technology, market, economic

- Public health disruptions, e.g., a global/regional health pandemic

- State disruptors, which are threats both physical and digital from foreign governments that may not agree with the policy of your organization or government

Enterprise Structure

When exploring the BOM, it is important to consider the structure of the organization, which may have evolved over decades and may now not be fit for purpose, requiring a restructure to service the new needs.

The structural analysis of the organization begins by exploring existing macro corporate structures, followed by a subsequent drill down into the lines of business, exploring the flows of information between these entities.

Enterprise structures should be compared to similar organizations in the industry and could represent a potential target for new optimized structures. All options should be considered, including outsourcing basic repeatable processes if cost effective.

Understanding the structure of the enterprise, both the physical and logical, provides us with the opportunity to analyze how any state changes will impact the current and future demand for services.

The larger the organization, often the more complex the enterprise structure.

Business Models

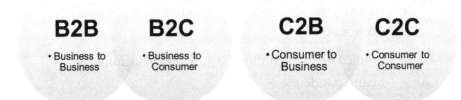

B2B
- Business to Business

B2C
- Business to Consumer

C2B
- Consumer to Business

C2C
- Consumer to Consumer

Figure 3-5. *Example business models*

A business model, as mentioned previously, is different from the business operating model and seeks to deliver the organizational charter, in that it captures, creates, and delivers value, using both internal and external instruments.

The business model will drive the structure, conduct, and overall performance of the organization, subject to the resources that are available and consumed, to deliver its services.

Business models are not dynamic and do not change often. However, disruptions do occur, and transformations are often driven by forces such as new entrants, innovations, or other factors, e.g., the arrival of a new CEO who wants to modify the raison d'être of the organization. When change occurs, it is rapid and a response to a disruptor.

Figure 3-5 illustrates various examples of macro-level business models, a useful tool for analyzing business models is the business model canvas (BMC), discussed in the following text, which describes the economic, social, cultural, and other contexts for analysis.

Information Resources

To deliver agile, relevant, and effective timely services, organizations need to appreciate and understand their information needs, i.e., the information held and consumed by the organization.

Understanding the macro-level information flows internally and externally to the organization is important. However, if economically viable, it may be prudent to deep dive and explore the informal flows of information, i.e., information that is not used in any specific process yet provides hidden value. This analysis of informal flows can add value to understanding the organizational BOM.

Organizations pull, consume, mold, and push information and services in one form or another. The insights derived from analysis of the flows, context, and usage of information can in many cases provide an advantage over its competitors when optimized and used proactively.

Two important questions to address during any analysis in relation to information resources for the BOM are as follows:

- How and what are the monetary drivers/cost (if quantifiable) for the production and delivery of information and the associated resources that are being pulled into the organization from third parties? This we determine through analysis of the physical and logical linkages between core information objects.

- Can the information be aggregated to provide insights of value, into patterns of behavior, that we can leverage to add critical value to our existing services and business activities?

Financial Management

The financial health and the organizational funding for projects and programs of work are important elements of the BOM. In lean times, the downstream effect on any technology initiatives will be constrained, as the organization will focus on keeping the lights on, i.e., avoid developing any system capabilities. So, it is important when planning the introduction or a technology change programs to have an appreciation of the financial position over the life of the program.

Information regarding the financial health of your organization or its competitors can be easily found through analysis of annual reports and market analysts (Bloomberg, Reuters, etc.).

There is a wealth of publicly available information produced by the large management consultancies, the likes of Ernst & Young, PwC, Deloitte, McKinsey, etc., which supply a vast amount information in the form of statistics, trend reports, industry analysis, etc. These sources of information provide key indicators of industry status and behaviors, but more importantly information on competitors such as the following:

- *Capital management*: Equity capital, debt capital, and specialty can be reviewed in the BOM to gauge an appreciation of the financial stability of the organization.

- *Funding*: The day-to-day operational cash flow and access to funding for projects for capital expenditure can be reviewed.

- *Reporting*: This includes the accounting-based reporting systems.

- *Ownership*: This includes the shareholding details.

- *Controls*: This includes the mechanism of financial controls and any limits on spend.

Tools/Methods

The previous considerations provide a baseline that should be considered when analyzing a BOM. There is, however, a set of tried and tested tools, methods, ad techniques that are available to provide an understanding of the organization in relation to its industry. We discuss the most popular methods, which are well-documented elsewhere and presented here for awareness.

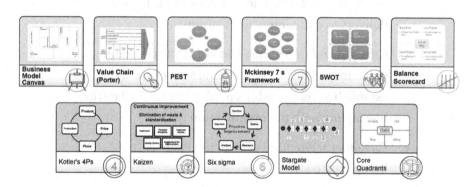

Figure 3-6. *Example tools/methods*

The Business Model Canvas

The business model canvas is one of those great visual tools that provides a simplistic macro view of how a business creates and delivers value for the stakeholders. The canvas is a great tool to frame the analysis of an organization with the following attributes laid out for inspection:

- *Key partners*: Analysis by identification of key partners and suppliers of the organization, i.e., who the organization interacts with

- *Key activities*: The activities that support and deliver the value proposition of the organization to its consumers

- *Key resources*: Required to service the value propositions of the organization

- *Value propositions*: The value the organization delivers to consumers or customers

- *Customer relationships*: The expectations of the consumer of the organizational services and the established relationships in play between all parties interacting with the organization

- *Customer segments*: For who the value is being created

- *Channels*: Representing the methods and tools used to serviced consumer needs

- *Cost structures*: Representing the costs in the business model

- *Revenue streams*: The value the customers are
  willing to pay for the consumption of the products
  or services

Templates of a blank canvas are available from our website and are a great tool to explore the nine key areas of your organization to provide insight into your existing model.

The BMC, as the name suggests, is a structured canvas with the aim to stimulate creativity and is suitable for the analysis and development of both existing and new business models.

Structure – Conduct – Performance (SCP)

The SCP is a well-established approach in industrial economics and used to analyze and understand industry characteristics.

In the SCP model, the conduct of firms is dependent on the structure of the market (size/distribution of competing firms), which has an impact on its overall performance. The three variables (SCP) each have an influence on the outcomes faced by the organization. Figure 3-7 illustrates this.

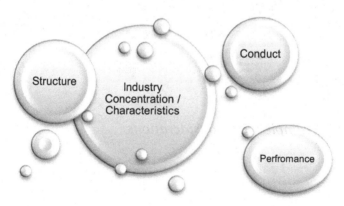

Figure 3-7. *Structure, conduct, performance*

SCP highlights market concentration, where a high degree of concentration will result in more market power thus resulting in an ability to set price above market conditions to earn supernormal profits.

For further information, see *Managerial Economics* (Bingham, Shipley).

PEST Analysis

Political, economic, social, and technological (PEST) is often used to track/ monitor and evaluate macro-economic environmental factors that may impact the organization now and in the future.

The framework supports the examination of opportunities and threats in relation to current and future political, economic, social, and technological forces that will impact the organization and is thus targeted at understanding the exposure by "big picture" forces of change and from this extrapolate any possible advantage of the opportunities that they present. Figure 3-8 depicts some examples.

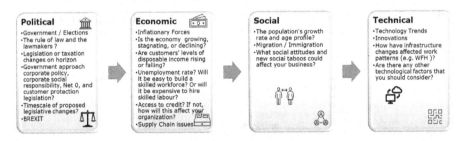

Figure 3-8. *Example PEST considerations*

SWOT Analysis

Strengths, weakness, opportunities, and threats (SWOT) analysis is a well-understood, well-documented self-assessment tool for matching capabilities and resources to the competitive environment in which the organization is operating in.

SWOT analysis is often used by many organizations as a strategic decision-making tool. Presented in a four-square grid (Figure 3-9), it highlights the highest weighted factors that can impact the organizational operations in the industry where strengths and weakness are perceived as internal to the organization and the threats/opportunities are seen coming from outside the organization and in some cases internal as well.

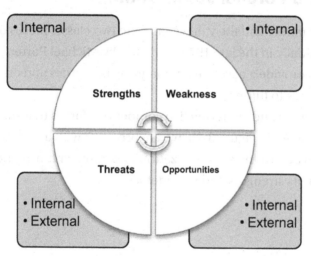

Figure 3-9. *SWOT*

SWOT can be summed up as follows:

- *Strengths*: The key strengths are the things the organization does well and includes especially any unique selling properties that the organization or function leverages.

- *Weaknesses*: What does the organization lack or not do well?

- *Opportunities*: These are opportunities that we can exploit to gain an advantage (commercial, operational, or tactical), e.g., technological, partnerships, channels, etc.

- *Threats*: This includes what is on the horizon that we should consider, e.g., changes in regulations, substitutes, net zero, pandemic, etc.

Porter's: 5 Forces/Value Chain

The 5 Forces model and the value chain[2] are two classic pieces of work, presented initially in the late 1970s early 80s by Michael Porter. They have continued to provide a baseline for analyzing industries and organizational competitiveness to this day.

By identifying and analyzing five competitive forces that shape an industry, depicted in Figure 3-10, we are provided with a foundation and framework to determine an organization's position within an industry together with its strengths and weaknesses.

---

[2] A value chain is a set of activities, where value is shown to be created or added, that a firm operating in a specific industry performs to deliver a service or product to a market.

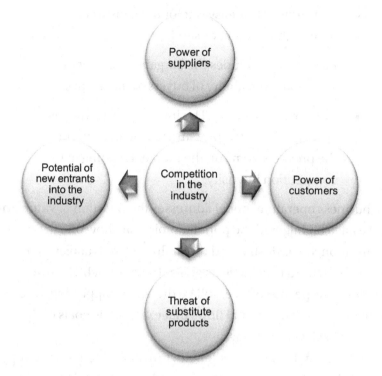

Figure 3-10. Porter's 5 Forces

The analysis helps assess industry attractiveness, how trends will affect industry competition, which industries a company should compete in, and how companies can position themselves for success.

The five forces comprise the following elements:

- *New entrants*: How easy is it for new entrants to enter or capture a stake in the market, what are the barriers to entry, and what are the associated threats that can arise from this?

- *Suppliers*: The bargaining power of suppliers is important especially in relation to setting any price points.

- *Substitutes*: How easy is it for the consumer to replace the product or service?

- *Buyers*: This includes the bargaining power of buyers and the ability of buyers to dictate price.

- *Industry competitors*: The intensity of a rivalry is represented by the pressure placed in terms of the previous items on the market resulting in the competition intensity.

The business operating model addresses the question of **value and being**. We have highlighted the popular tools that allow one to understand the organization, the industry, and the multiple forces at play to move organizations forward to achieve its goals. To deliver a BOM, every organization, irrespective of size, will be driven by supporting processes, i.e., the network of transactional flows that execute the goals of the BOM, which is the next layer to discuss.

The value chain is well-documented, providing a lens on the support and primary business processes starting with a core that represents a set of activities that an organization carries out to create value, and this general-purpose value chain allows companies to examine all their activities and see how they're connected.

Through the value chain we seek to provide insights into the effectiveness of numerous chains of activities when broken down and explore the effectiveness of each value stream of the activities.

When aggregated and compared with similar organizations, we can analyze/measure existing activities that provide us with that competitive edge that we want to maintain.

Figure 3-11 highlights the value chain with a few example activities listed that would provide a baseline for further analysis.

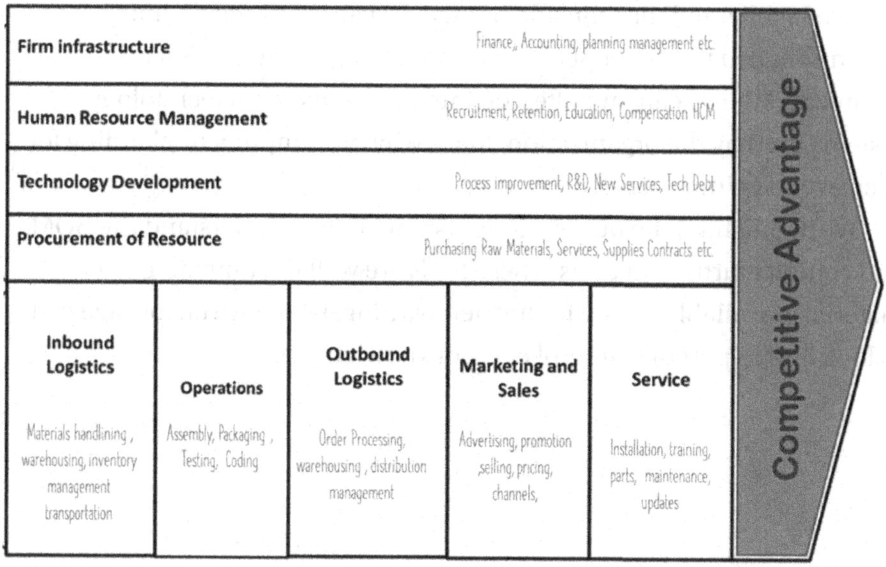

Firm infrastructure	Finance, Accounting, planning management etc.	
Human Resource Management	Recruitment, Retention, Education, Compensation HCM	
Technology Development	Process improvement, R&D, New Services, Tech Debt	
Procurement of Resource	Purchasing Raw Materials, Services, Supplies Contracts etc.	

Inbound Logistics	Operations	Outbound Logistics	Marketing and Sales	Service
Materials handlining , warehousing, inventory management transportation	Assembly, Packaging , Testing, Coding	Order Processing, warehousing , distribution management	Advertising, promotion ,selling, pricing, channels,	Installation, training, parts, maintenance, updates

Competitive Advantage

Figure 3-11. *The value chain*

We have discussed just some of the many analysis models that are available. All are well-documented and provide tools for architects.

However, there are numerous other frameworks and models that provide a structure for analyzing resources, processes, practices, and your business models.

Summary

In this chapter, we explored layer 0, i.e., the business operating model of the stack introduced in the previous chapter.

Layer 0, it was shown, can be subdivided into two focus areas that aid architectural thinking, i.e., considerations and tools.

We highlighted that considerations will vary between organizations and introduced the concept of drivers for change, which affect all organizations and can and often do impact downstream technology systems used by the organization; that's why pre-empting or planning for such events is important.

We highlighted the numerous tools available to understand the BOM and conduct further analysis. These tools are well documented, and material is available online for further learning, which we encourage you to look into as part of your tool chest of knowledge.

CHAPTER 4

Layer 1: Business Process Layer

As previously discussed, the business operating model (BOM) establishes the organizational sense of purpose, i.e., its *raison d'être*. This sense of purpose can be realized through a set of supporting and enabling layers subject to constraints. The first of such layers is the process layer, which is a layer that adopts a lean, agile, cost-effective, and efficiency-driven characteristic to deliver value. Hence, it is important to understand, at a macro and in some cases a micro level, how these processes when orchestrated deliver the operational, support, and management services to the BOM.

Processes found in the process layer can be divided into three variations.

- *Core* processes represent, at a minimum, the individual tasks to be accomplished to achieve a certain level of uniformity in output, without consideration to any underlying resources (people, technology, etc.). For example, "take order" can be executed as simply by writing on a piece of paper the order or as complex as capture via an order entry system. However, irrespective of approach, this is still an essential process in the sales lifecycle that must be captured and understood.

© Daljit Roy Banger 2022
D. R. Banger, *Enterprise Systems Architecture*,
https://doi.org/10.1007/978-1-4842-8646-3_4

- *Guiding* processes are used as guardrails in the design and governance of the organization. In some cases, these processes may be dictated in part and audited by third parties, e.g., evidence of identity checks, which may be part of a regulatory requirement for finance companies.

- *Enabling* processes provide for the fulfilment of a core business process and subsequent delivery of capabilities, e.g., IT service delivery, marketing, HR, etc.

A process, in general, will have a start and a finish and deliver some "outcome of value" when executed or orchestrated, which can be manually or via some digital means. A process can be completed, paused, triggered, or spawn a subprocess that may return a value to enable the main process to continue, if the logic permits.

When considering a business process, the first impulse is to treat it as a single, monolithic, sequential process executed by an individual (person), a digital enabler (robot), or a mechanical device, which is not always the case.

Let us consider a simple process, one that is often perceived as a sequential one: "take card payment." This is something that on the face of it looks uncomplicated. However, on closer examination, we see additional complexity in the transparent background, dependencies, and triggers that are driven by one or many subprocesses.

1. The cashier enters the amount on the credit card terminal and asks the customer to tap their card on the terminal.

2. This digital information is sent to the payment processes that authorize the payment with the card's network.

3. After the payment has been authorized, it needs
    to be authenticated. The card's network sends the
    information needed to confirm the card's legitimacy
    to the customer's issuing bank.

4. The bank verifies that the card is being used
    legitimately and has access to the funds or credit
    card limit required to complete the sale and then
    either approves or declines the transaction.

5. This then completes the sale in the store. However,
    additional processes are initiated, e.g., updating the
    accounting systems (sales, general ledgers, etc.).

This list, while a simple explanation of a complex set of flows,
illustrates how processes are seldomly sequential; i.e., they can spawn
single or multiple sets of subprocesses during execution, which in
some cases may not permit completion due to dependencies on this
downstream process.

However, there are several well-defined common processes that span
multiple industries to support and simplify business capabilities that can
be found in most commercial e-business systems. For example, enterprise
resource planning (ERP) systems leverage *pre-canned* workflows, such as
supply chain management (SCM), customer relationship management
(CRM), sales, and finance, that come with multiple preconfigured
subprocesses, e.g., procure to pay, order to cash (OTC), etc.

Figure 4-1 depicts a simple process chain, in which the flow cannot
complete successfully until results from downstream subprocesses are
completed. These types of process maps visually depict chains, flows,
dependencies, and associations and can be used to explore efficiency
savings as they can emphasize options for change and the subsequent
impacts where procedures are removed, broken, or reconfigured.

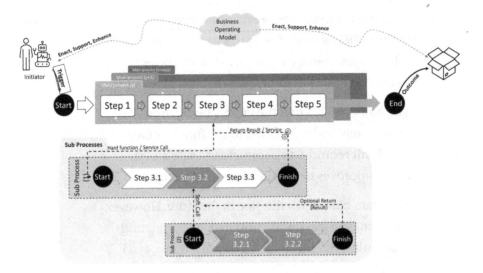

Figure 4-1. *Sequential process flow spawning subprocesses*

The ability to visualize business and system processes is one of the core skills of an EA. EAs should be able to present a set of processes, activities, or lists in a simplistic graphical way that highlights flow and potential impacts if any. Let us consider the following simple list of process steps:

- Take the order.

- Check the availability.

- Take payment.

- Dispatch item.

- Notify the customer of the delivery date/time.

- Move the goods.

- Receive the goods in the local delivery hub.

- The customer receives goods.

- Perform any post-sales activity.

The previous is a basic list of steps, and you can obtain an appreciation for the overall steps in the process flow; however, what we lack is judgmental clarity in terms of events and any associated actions.

If we now present the same information as a simple graphical flow (Figure 4-2), we observe additional implied context. In essence, we use the list information but now present it visually as a simple process map.

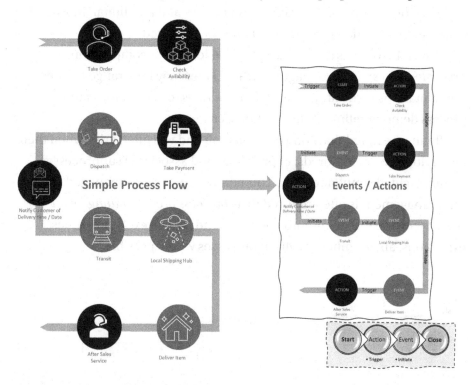

Figure 4-2. *Level 0 process flow: context with implied actions and events*

Figure 4-2 represents what we refer to as a *level 0 flow*. These high-level diagrams present sufficient information to allow the audience to appreciate the overall flow, links, and dependencies in the process chain.

As previously mentioned, EAs need to be conversant with the creation and presentation of level 0 process diagrams, as these provide a powerful tool for the presentation of simple concepts, where the use of notations remains flexible, due to the nature of the audience and the context presented.

However, when moving to the next level of decomposition, i.e., level 0, formal methods and notational standards should be adopted, as the audience of the process diagrams now changes and additional information (rules, triggers, actions, events, etc.) must be rendered.

Figure 4-3 depicts a flowchart, the next level of decomposition, presented as a *swim lane* diagram, where lanes may be arranged either horizontally or vertically and each lane belongs to each actor in the process demonstrating the interactions, etc.

It must be noted that complications can and will often arise when there are multiple, even hundreds, of processes and associated subprocesses being executed simultaneously. This complexity must be managed, and this management is often referred to as *business process management* (BPM) with the goal to monitor, manage, and reduce execution times, exceptions, and number of call-off processes where possible.

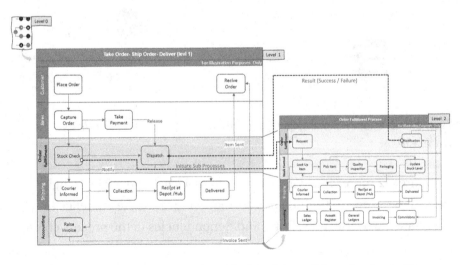

Figure 4-3. *Decomposition example level 1 and 2 swim lane diagram*

In this figure we have highlighted the importance of visualization, which is important and crucial in understanding and delivering lean processes. However, there are two core elements to a business process that the architect must consider when analyzing processes.

- *Process definition*: Although not a true part of the stack mapping, it must be understood, as processes will be defined and then further optimized as new capabilities emerge and the BOM changes.

- *Process execution*: This is important, as one needs to be aware of how a process is executed, what the start and end positions are, and what the triggers are. This is important to allow mapping between the BOM and the capabilities layers below.

Although definition and execution are important in real terms, processes must be qualified, quantified, and mapped to a use case[1] and then documented or captured prior to any optimization or execution.

The life cycle associated with process analysis and definition can be summed up as follows:

- *Analysis* of use cases, identification of any gas and the detection of areas for improvement which drive the desired BOM outcomes is essential. Principles, such as Ockham's razor,[2] are applied during this stage with a drive to capture, identify, measure and exploration of process interactions to identify where value can be added or gained.

---

[1] A use case is a story relating to a specific situation or requirement in which a product or service could potentially be used.

[2] Ockham's razor is a simple problem-solving principle which states "Entities should not be multiplied without necessity and that all other things being equal, simpler explanations are generally better than more complex ones."

- *Design* is the product of the analysis and is used to design (if new) or redesign (if inefficient) processes. This will include the notational representation of the processes, e.g., BPMN swim lane designs and all subprocess interfaces/interactions built out.

- *Optimized* refers to the "build" and the associated optimization of the process in terms of duration at runtime and the associated cost of execution.

- *Socialization* is required to ensure that compliance and process execution is efficiently adopted and executed through the user and stakeholder community.

- *Execution* is the actual test and operation of the processes, in a runtime environment, where execution can be a manual or robotic/automated system driven.

- *Maintenance* is required to ensure the ongoing integrity of the process and that the process continues to adhere to the original principles of design.

These stages and flows are represented in Figure 4-4 as a sequence of steps. However, it should be noted that as the requirements of the BOM change, so will the processes or the orchestration steps required.

Figure 4-4. *Process life cycle*

- **Notations**

Capturing and documenting business and systems processes is both time-consuming and labor-intensive. To speed up the process, many tools exist that facilitate a move from a visual representation model (drop/drag/ design) to stub (code) generation, which allows reduced effort as new processes are incorporated or identified, thus speeding up the development/execution operations lifecycle.

Communities in the form of user groups, individuals, or industry specialists come together to define standards for notations specific to their industry. These standards can be shared and used across the industry to support analysis, collaboration, description, and visualization of architectures within and across business domains in an unambiguous way. Three good examples of notational standards are as follows:

- Business Process Model and Notation (BPMN) was developed by the Object Management Group (`http://www.bpmn.org`).

- The Unified Modeling Language (UML) is a general-purpose, developmental modeling language intended to provide a standard way to visualize both structural and behavioral elements in the design of a system (`http://uml.org`).

- Archimate is a technical standard from the Open Group and can be considered an aggregation of popular notational standards with concepts of the IEEE 1471 standard (`https://www.opengroup.org/ archimate-forum`).

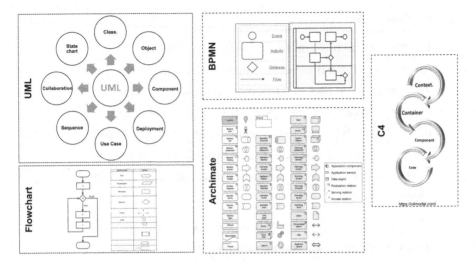

Figure 4-5. *Publicly available notational standards*

Layer 1: BOM Analysis Considerations

The following is a list of considerations that should be considering when reviewing and analyzing the business process layer:

- *Process type*

  a. Manual

  Often basic processes, which require simple executions and are initialized by a human, require zero-level automation in which every process will start and end in a short execution window.

  Manual processes should be measurable/quantifiable and add value to the organization value flows, and the event could be either an internal or external trigger.

The processes should create or execute a value enabler, i.e., something that provides value directly or indirectly to the BOM.

Note that prior to automating any process, one should seek to improve it, i.e., reduce existing inefficiencies.

b.   Automatic

Automatic processes are, as the name suggests, automatic. Once triggered, they require no manual intervention and through the process lifecycle may trigger multiple events. These robotic processes may "spawn" multiple processes, which can also be scheduled to meet a future point-in-time objective.

Robotic process automation (RPA) is a software technology that makes it easy to build, deploy, and manage software robots that emulate human actions interacting with digital systems and software.

Some generic questions one should ask during process analysis are as follows:

- *How* does the process or "processes journey" support a specific use case, which in turn supports the business operating model?

- *How* are the processes executed, e.g., via a manual mechanism such as the push of a button or automated and triggered via a set of robotic processes executed at a specific time, stage, or within an alternate subprocess?

- *What* triggers exist, manual or automatic, that initiate the process, and how are these implemented?

- Is there a clear entry/exit criterion for processes; i.e., can a process be halted or terminated due to no completion, and if so, what is the impact or rollback measures?

- Are level 0 processes assigned to individuals or groups of activities?

- Who/what are the process custodians/owners?

- *Formal/informal execution*

  It is important to capture any rules associated with a process; e.g., if a process requires you to contact a third party to initiate a dialogue and request information, then it becomes important to understand the exchange mechanism rules, such as data/information exchange protocols to understand the nature of the exchange, e.g., formal agreed-upon technique or something that is ad hoc and informal.

  The capture of the context, surrounding the rules, which drive the design of processes is crucial when considering potential reuse or extensibility of said processes across the enterprise.

- *Straight through/call off flow*

  In most cases, processes are generally executed in sequence, unless there is a quality gate that requires a process output to be validated, authenticated, or quality controlled and then re-submitted upon failure, or there are multiple threads for spawn processes. Either way, processes tend to be sequential and executed in a straight-through fashion.

There are, however, instances when a process needs to call to a dependent third party that controls a discrete activity. For example, in the manufacture and assembly of automobiles, it is common practice for global companies to build/assemble engines away from the main assembly line and pull them in, adopting a just-in-time approach when required on the assembly process.

No business is static, and thus it would be prudent to ensure, when designing processes, that clear separation/loose coupling is a core principle that is adopted.

- *Outsourced*

   We have seen, in the past two decades, a move to outsource simple back-end business services that are scriptable, measurable, and repeatable to both offshore and near-shore destinations. This is often justified by the argument that this enables organizations to focus on their core offering/services.

   Initially the justification for outsourcing both systems and processes were centred on financial savings. However, this argument has subsided in recent years and the focus has shifted from *cost* to *quality* with financial economies downgraded in the decision making process.

   This "outsource" model requires processes to be clearly articulated, integration points defined, and the process mechanism to be analyzed prior to any execution.

- *Execution*

    Process execution is critical to delivering the BOM
    requirements. This execution should be robust,
    speedy, agile, optimized, and cost effective, which is
    only truly possible if adequate process measurements
    and controls are in place.

    Any robotic micro tasking while encapsulated in
    the macro process should be considered a separate
    process and thus treated as a call-off process subject
    to relevance.

    It is important to differentiate between process
    orchestration and choreography when exploring
    execution as highlighted in Figure 4-6 below.

Process Orchestration entails actively **controlling all elements and interactions** in the process chain similar to that of a conductor who directs the musicians of an orchestra.

 Process choreography entails establishing a **pattern or routine** that are followed as the music plays, without requiring supervision and instructions.

Figure 4-6. *Orchestration vs. choreography*

We have discussed some of the core concepts that drive the business
process layer, a layer whose primary focus is to enable and support
the BOM.

The analysis and design should encapsulate the following:

- Elaborating on and defining both automatic and manual processes to identify the following:

    - The processes that support the BOM

    - Triggers for the start/end process and how are they executed

    - Entry/exit criteria

    - Robotic process automation

    - Process custodians

- Analyzing the process flows and chains to identify the straight-through or call-off process

    - Process threading

    - Process flow

    - Orchestrations

- Exploring the process execution cycles

    - Can any processes be better optimized by third parties, outsourced at a lower unit cost

    - The measurement/control of process cycles

    - Deep diving into micro tasking

    - Optimization, current and future; the maximum value through using minimum processes to add value

- Exploring the design and redesign

    - Visualization of these process must use a standard notational representation

Summary

In this chapter, we explored layer 1, i.e., the business process layer, which supports the BOM by orchestrating all the services and capabilities required to achieve the desired organizational outcomes.

Process analysis, design, and management are substantial topics, and we introduced the key elements and the notational standards available to use in designs.

All the key topics are summarized in Figure 4-7.

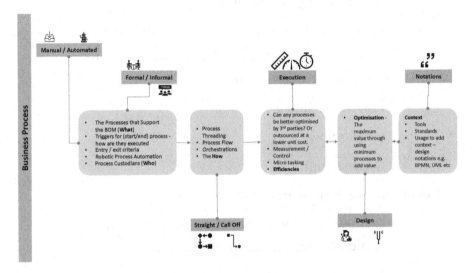

Figure 4-7. Process layer analysis

CHAPTER 5

Layer 2: Capabilities and Services

In the previous section, we introduced the process layer. This layer is positioned between the business operating model and all subsequent layers and drives the activity that ensures that the support and outcomes are delivered.

Layer 2 represents the capabilities and services that provide a generic contextual grouping with structures. This targets the ability to orchestrate process, business, and systems functions via the execution of abstract services, managing the execution of the underlying system functionality.

This layer acts as a proxy between the business and technical layers, allowing a decoupling between technical (systems) or business capabilities. This can then be executed/orchestrated to meet both tactical (point-in-time) or strategic outcomes.

> *A capability is a logical representation of a set of core business functions that map to the BOM, as opposed to a service that provides the ability to do something or deliver something of material value.*

Human capital management (HCM), required for the management of employees, is a good example of a business capability that is centered around the functions for employee management. This logically encapsulates services such as payroll, pensions, recruitment, starters, and leavers. This business capability has rules, processes, and procedures that

© Daljit Roy Banger 2022
D. R. Banger, *Enterprise Systems Architecture*,
https://doi.org/10.1007/978-1-4842-8646-3_5

allow the management of employees and any of the associated compliance obligations required by law.

Capabilities are represented, as one would expect, as nouns, like *human capital management.* Processes are named with verbs, as they describe an action or occurrence, like *operate the payroll.*

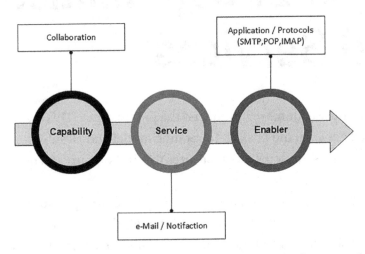

Figure 5-1. *Process: capability service execution with example*

It is important to note that in essence a capability maps to one or many services, which in turn can execute one or more system enablers or micro services.

Capabilities, when classified, created, and mapped back to the BOM, help represent an overview and landscape of the enterprise. These capability maps, when segmented or classified depending on the audience can aid, as well as support, business and investment planning, where investing in core capabilities may deliver the greatest value to the organization, e.g., the segmentation by core and noncore capabilities that can prioritize resources.

At a systems level, the service layer introduces a concept of intrinsic interoperability and loose coupling between the application layer and the process layer, in which a capability can be delivered by executing one or more services required to facilitate that process.

Figure 5-2 illustrates the "separation" between the process and enablers. Process A may act as an individual discrete process or form part of a wider process chain that supports the BOM and calls a business capability via a controller, which in turn invokes a service. A service or group of micro services exists to support one or many business processes and are delivered by either using, parsing, or exploiting specific systems enablers.

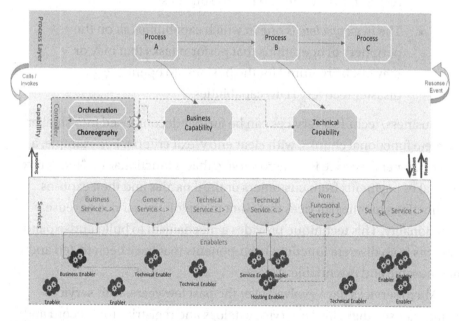

Figure 5-2. *Process to service/enabler flow*

A key role of an enterprise architect is to deliver/develop a set of capability models, which represent a clear understanding of the business needs for a particular domain and can represented in multiple ways. The following are examples:

- The *business view* represents business capabilities that define business-specific domains, such as selling, buying, inventory management, and support for various process journeys like procure to pay, order to cash, etc.

- The *operational view* represents the capabilities required to operate and run the business.

- The *hygiene view* is one in which capabilities sit on the periphery of operations that perform tasks that may or may not be required for the business to operate, e.g., disaster recovery (DR) capabilities.

Business/technical services can be further decomposed into smaller discrete functional chunks, with clear entry/exit criteria. For example, a "take payment" service is a micro service that is functionally a "black box" that takes payments from customers or third parties and then exposes its functions to other services that want to exploit the service or reuse functionality. This technique provides a mechanism to build and expand systems from discrete functional components that have been tested and so are reusable and extendable.

Micro services have evolved over the past few years, with services being exposed digitally via service catalogs and registries that record and expose clear execution points with the data being clearly bounded.

The extraction of capabilities is discussed further in the "Strategy" section later in the Chapter 15.

Capability/Service Layer Considerations

When exploring the organizational capabilities and developing various portfolio visuals that relate to the services, you may want to consider the following components and artifacts:

- *Controller*

Understanding how services are executed/invoked allows architects to appreciate and optimize the runtime characteristics, especially when services are invoked via an enterprise service bus (ESB) systems mechanism.

- *Capability classification*

There are no specific rules to classify or group capabilities; these are extraordinarily industry/ organization specific, but the following are some generic considerations one may want to adopt in their capability/service map analysis and development.

  - Core/noncore

  - Cost value relationships

  - Strategic, tactical, and operational benefits

  - Commodity (off the shelf/publicly available) resources

  - Internal/outsourced competencies

  - Core differentiators/innovating resources

- *Service catalogs*

The service catalog is the registry of all business and technical services. This will evolve over time as projects standardize and capture new services that are added and enable further consumption and may be extended to incorporate an application programming interface (API) catalog subject to the use case.

The index of micro capabilities/services are decomposed single reusable instances that are shared/exposed through the enterprise service catalog.

The catalog is similar to a product/inventory index listing services with syntax and characteristics showing how and when to use.

It should be noted that the IT Infrastructure Library (ITIL) views a service catalog as a structured repository holding information about all its services. The ITL service catalog forms part of the service portfolio published to clients/ users and is used to support the delivery of it services. This view is very much IT centric; however, it can be used to manage the service delivery to the supporting BOM.

- *Technical services*

Although the focus is on defining business services, it is important to capture the enablers that often are the technical execution services (e.g., calls to applications in layer 3). It is important to analyze the associated technical capabilities that deliver the services in support of the business processes and how these can be executed in a streamlined fashion to deliver value to the organization.

The costs associated with the provision of these services can be significant, so any downstream replication needs to be eradicated, which is best achieved by shared project policies and strict governance controls.

- *Tactical vs. operational*

It is important to ensure that capabilities and services either are defined as short-term tactical (throwaway) or are embedded through the long-term requirements.

Tactical services can be seen as "quick and dirty," i.e., developed as ad hoc nonstandard products to meet or service a point-in-time need.

- *Business*

Business capabilities are aligned to the BOM, as one would expect, where they are perceived as the implementation vehicle for the BOM. The capabilities can be classified as either formal and informal, where the latter is not bound to any specific rule set, however provide an intangible advantage to the organization when executed.

- *Innovation/industry disruptors*

Innovation as a capability is worthy of mention. It is an important *wrapper*, which supports the introduction for innovation within the capability matrix and can be seen to be bidirectional as this set of processes deliver capabilities either directly to the BOM or to the downstream organizational activities.

Several approaches to innovation exist, e.g., the Funnel,[1] which requires multiple capabilities to manage the innovation lifecycle, i.e., from inception to introduction and then finally execution.

It is also worth mentioning that, in some cases, unique developed capabilities may provide a competitive advantage to the organization at a point in time, where the capability challenges the existing industry mode of operation providing value in the form of first-move advantages in the industry due to the temporary disruption.

Channels

A channel, as a capability, can be contentious as one can argue it represents a delivery platform; however, we will include it so it is captured. Channels come in many shapes and sizes providing the ability to render and deliver services to internal, external, and third-party consumers. Examples of channels are, but not limited to, the following:

- Interactive voice response/recognition (IVR) services allow interaction between customers using voice and dual-tone multifrequency (DTMF) tones input via a phone keypad.

- Web/portals provide a customized web gateway or entry point into the organization, allowing the use of its services or exposing dynamic information exposed.

---

[1] The innovation capability supports a funnel management process, which in most organizations seeks to provide the mechanism to enable a constant stream of ideas that are screened for viability in terms of cost and value to ensure that the company can create realistic introduction plans for innovation.

- Fixed kiosks are hardware terminals, i.e., fixed devices, often in public places, that allow interaction with the public and often are used to provide basic information or services to the public or a defined segment of users.

- Electronic mail as a channel is a wrapper for a set of mail protocol services.

- An API is a protocol-defined interface between two or more systems with the exchange of information between them, intended to standardize and simplify data interchange between applications.

- Web or Internet services use the various protocols to perform set functions on agreed upon ports, e.g., Secure File Transfer Protocol (SFTP), which usually runs on port 22 and is a way to transfer files between machines over a secure and encrypted connection.

- Television which is commonly used by organizations exploiting specialist 'shopping channels' to promote or sell a product or service.

- Gaming platforms enable certain services to be provisioned by leveraging the underlying platform and targeting a specific market.

- Pervasive devices e.g., mobile phones which provide tailored customer journeys to perform real-time transactions on trusted appliances.

- Social media services are often exposed using dynamic platforms.

- Collaboration services are services that support the sharing of information and data in workflows among a group internal or external to the organization.

Example Mapping: Automobile Industry

In Figure 5-3, we illustrate a basic capability-service-enablement linkage by exploring common capabilities found in the automobile manufacturing industry.

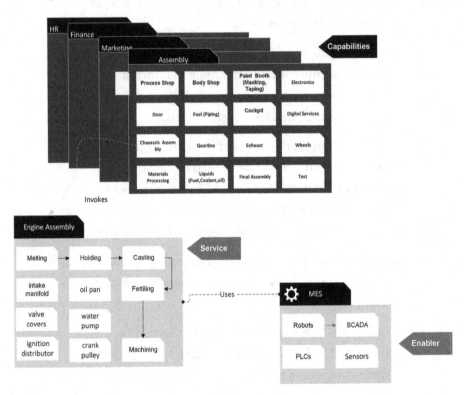

Figure 5-3. *Capability-service-enablement*

The preliminary stage in capability analysis is to define a level 1 set of capabilities found in the organization, e.g., HR, marketing, finance. In our example, for simplicity, we have excluded several important capabilities, e.g., logistics, distribution, dealerships, etc. Under normal circumstances, when conducting a capability inventory/map, one would include and represent all high-level capabilities found in the organization.

During this initial analysis, it would be sensible to identify the next-level capabilities. For example, if we explore automobile assembly as a level 1 capability, we observe several continual capabilities, e.g., exhaust assembly, which we refer to as level 2.

In essence, a level 1 capability such as "assembly" would have one or many subcapabilities, e.g., door, cockpit, and axles. All would require assembly to the main vehicle on a production line.

The "chassis assembly" capability, as one would expect, calls multiple services, such as the "engine assembly," and encapsulates numerous subservices, e.g., the engine casting service where manufacturers cast raw materials like a melting/molding service and maybe additional bespoke services like the inclusion of water pumps.

All the previous services, as they run along the production line process, will require the enablement of various computerized systems. For example, a manufacturing execution system (MES) may involve the asset of robots or supervisory control and data acquisition (SCADA) systems, etc. The MES may service one or more capabilities; e.g., the MES will be used in the final assembly and gearbox assembly.

The previous, in brief, illustrates how the assembly capability leverages multiple services, e.g., engine assembly, which in turn requires the enablers to provide the execution capabilities.

Summary

Capabilities and services provide a *separation of concerns* between the process layer and the downstream enablers.

Capabilities when consolidated into a single inventory provide a map of the things the business does and needs to service the BOM and can be used as a decision-making tool for investment and resource allocation.

Services and micro services act as the enablers for the capabilities and can be segmented into either business or technical services and decomposed further for clarity.

Tactical, operational, and innovation capabilities are not static; hence, they require constant recalibration for alignment to the needs of the to the BOM. For example, in our automobile example, if we include a shift from fossil fuels to electric, then the original capability map would be drastically altered to include a battery assembly and eliminate gas/diesel-related set of functions.

Services can be further decomposed and can if required be treated as "black box" services where the internals of the service are invisible to the consumer of that service.

Figure 5-4 summarizes the key considerations when analyzing layer 2.

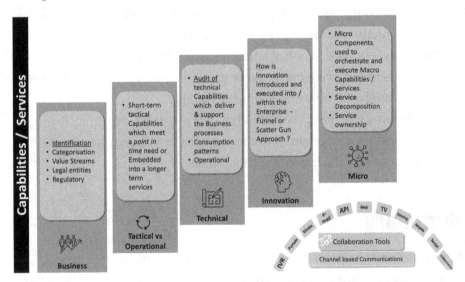

Figure 5-4. *Considerations for capabilities/services*

CHAPTER 6

Layer 3: Applications

The application layer represents the attributes, taxonomy, and portfolio of actual computer programs that provide digital enablement for delivering the capabilities, workflow, and services via the service and process layers to the BOM.

The process layer controls the workflows that leverage one or many services that invoke an application or segment of its functionality, a module, a component, or simply an API call that on processing returns data or results up through the chain to the controlling workflow process.

In organizations with large application inventories, i.e., several hundreds of applications, there is a strong requirement to structure the planning, introduction, management, and control of all applications and any associated subcomponents. This task is often assigned to an enterprise architect responsible for applications, one who understands the various components in the application landscape and any potential vulnerabilities during the lifecycle of the application.

How applications are procured, developed, and managed represents a complex set of tasks especially in a multidimensional complex ecosystem, and the need to understand lower-level application components, interactions, and integrations becomes important to deliver the measurement, control, and maintenance in a cost-effective way that ultimately supports and facilitates the BOM.

© Daljit Roy Banger 2022
D. R. Banger, *Enterprise Systems Architecture*,
https://doi.org/10.1007/978-1-4842-8646-3_6

Figure 6-1 illustrates a common pattern, where multiple internal services call applications that may be hosted on third-party cloud locations. These internal applications are routed via a proxy application or channel that is responsible for maintaining a trust relationship between parties.

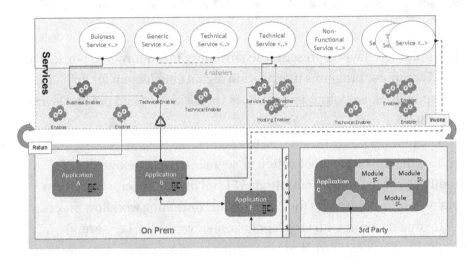

Figure 6-1. *Service to application flow*

The application estate in Figure 6-1 presents a simple view. However, the applications are hosted or provisioned in disparate physical locations and supplied by a single or multiple vendors, implementing the application as a service (AaaS) model. The complexity in this application model gives rise to several concerns such as the security, latency, and integrity of transactions.

Previously, organizations relied on a single monolithic application suite that supported the BOM and met nearly all the requirements, as was the case in the 1970s, 80s, and 90s, where companies like IBM sold the physical hardware and software supporting all functions and where managing the IT landscape was relatively calm. However, with a move to a distributed federated and decoupled set of systems, we now find this management (especially when operations are distributed across the globe, operating in different time zones, and deployed in geographically dispersed data centers) has become more complicated in terms of management and service delivery.

At the application layer, it is vital we understand the value streams around the management of the application landscape, i.e., how applications are procured, constructed, integrated, deployed, and managed. It's also important to understand the cost of ownership to ensure we deliver efficient value for the money to the business and meet all the BOM objectives and outcomes.

Components to Analyze, Consider, and Manage in the Application Layer

The application layer has many aspects that need to be considered to deliver an efficient, lean, cost-effective service to the enterprise. Here are some factors to consider when analyzing and exploring the application layer:

- *Reference architectures/standards*

  To avoid constantly re-inventing the wheel, meaning the architecture, the community has produced reference architectures and standards. These artifacts are then used as reusable, repeatable, tested design patterns to provide high-level insights, guardrails, and best practices for organizing system components.

  The reference architectures must not be confused with reference systems as they provide data/information and cite sources in a standardized way for consumers. A good example of a system is a ZIP code system that manages post codes and exposes this information as static data objects to consumer systems.

Level 0 (top-level) reference architectures are often presented in high-level design (HLD) documents and provide context for the system landscape. This is a common artifact that encapsulates core processes and capabilities required to deliver the desired outcomes.

The new cloud, aka hosting, offerings such as Google Cloud Platform (GCP), Amazon Web Services (AWS), Alibaba Cloud and Azure from Microsoft all provide reference architecture documents/diagrams supporting transition to the platforms with additional knowledge transfer and deployment notes.

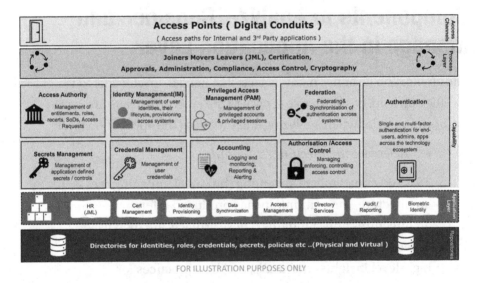

Figure 6-2. *Example level 0 reference architecture for an IAM architecture*

Figure 6-2 illustrates a typical example of a reference architecture diagram, in this case for identity and access management, which can be found in many large enterprises. We have kept this very generic for illustration purposes but are highlighting common capabilities in reference architecture that can provide a reusable pattern.

- The top layer represents access points, i.e., the points of entrance to the digital ecosystem. It is important to stress that this must encapsulate the path for third-party systems that access the organizational systems.

- The process layer outlines the workflows in the identify and access management (IAM) domain that connects the identified processes with the technical capabilities.

- The capabilities define individual services required in the IAM reference architecture. These capabilities can represent numerous security controls that are used to secure data, applications, and infrastructure or features that support the various IAM-related processes. Capabilities are linked with polices, standards, principles, risks, threats, control requirements, and control objectives for full traceability, while others should include hygiene type services, e.g., accounting type services.

- Below the capabilities we find applications that underpin and support the IAM capabilities when orchestrated to deliver the enablers allowing access to data, etc.

- We include in our reference architecture the data layer, which delivers the information on existing directories for all identity and access-related information.

The example level 0 reference architecture is a common artifact found in many organizations. If you ask your enterprise security team, they may provide you with a similar, extended type reference architecture diagram for your enterprise.

Figure 6-2 provides a high-level context on the key processes, capabilities, and applications used to provide and support the BOM. However, this remains generic until we turn to the next level of decomposition, i.e., level 1 where we add some more detail and assign named applications or services to the domain diagram, as illustrated in Figure 6-3.

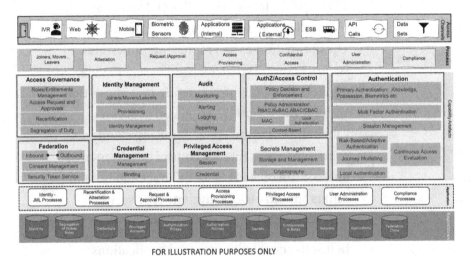

FOR ILLUSTRATION PURPOSES ONLY

Figure 6-3. *Example level 1 reference model*

Reference architecture can provide the "building blocks" for the creation of a reusable system constructs and when supported by the adoption of standards can provide consistency across the enterprise or industry.

88

Standards can act as the system guardrails for projects allowing architects to reuse and encapsulate these guidelines, best practices, programming styles, class libraries, and typo conventions to application developers who follow when developing source code. These standards allow structure and uniformity across a code base, resulting in reduced time to market and simplifying tasks of code maintenance and portability.

Standards come in many shapes and sizes as seen in two popular frameworks, i.e., the Jakarta EE [11], formerly Java EE and J2EE, and the .NET Framework [12] from Microsoft, both providing developers with a rich selection of specifications, class libraries, platform interoperability, and bespoke tools to develop applications that can be federated, distributed, or delivered as stand-alone applications.

- *Commercial-off-the-shelf (COTS)*

COTS software tends to support a specific business function or domain. Most COTS products are built and delivered by third-party software vendors, with the resources to support the product during its life. Salesforce, SAP, and Oracle are examples of such vendors that provide large complex enterprise resource planning (ERP) suites provisioned either on premise or via their cloud infrastructure.

COTS products comprise a suite of programs, which organizations can buy to serve a specific function in their industry. For example, an organization can purchase an order-to-cash (OTC[1]) module or a complete ERP product from the supplier. COTS packages are designed to meet a cradle-to-grave process activity.

COTS products should be treated as any other product on the application register, must be managed in terms of its product roadmap (functionality, versions, minor/major upgrades, etc.), and should provision for decommissioning. The real benefits are found in the underlying principle, where the need for the organization to maintain a development and support team becomes obsolete.

There are several questions that should be addressed when procuring a COTS package. These questions should ensure that all functional and nonfunctional and commercial requirements are met.

When considering a COTS product, it is important during the evaluation stage, to consider potential future decommissioning costs and how any data held in the system, will be removed into standard reusable format which is significant when adopting an Application as a Service (AaaS) model i.e., applications hosted in third-party physical environments.

---

[1] *Order-to-cash* (OTC) is a set of business processes to manage the lifecycle from sales order right through to customer payments.

- *Bespoke development*

COTS packages tend to be immutable, primarily due to the fact they are sold and designed for multiple customers. This model results in vendors attempting to capture generic requirements from multiple sources resulting in a gap for any single organization's needs against the offering. These gaps are often excluded from product roadmaps and thus must be filled through the development of bespoke code. This code must be developed, managed, and deployed.

Bespoke software development also occurs when there is not a COTS package function that can be reused, customized, or configured to meet a specific business requirement or address a specific BOM-related problem.

Bespoke development can be either an internally resourced piece of work or outsourced to a third-party development organization and can encapsulate the development of tailor-made software or micro service functionality that can either extend or plug in to an existing software framework or leverage component plugins or adaptors to allow for the integration of systems.

Bespoke development can take on many challenges, with the biggest one being of forward compatibility as new releases of the package become available and do not accommodate backward compatibility for the organization-developed code.

- *In-house/out-source*

Development can be undertaken either within a function of the organization using internal resources (in-house) else procured or outsourced to a third party with development capabilities. A consultancy or software house approach should consider the following factors:

- *Skills*: Does the organization have the skills available to undertake the project in-house, and are these skills proven?

- *Cost*: Consider all the costs including the opportunity cost (cost of the forgone alternative) relating to not only the guild and deployment, but also the ongoing cost of support.

- *Support*: Consider the support during the lifecycle of the product.

- *Delivery*: Does the organization have the skills to deliver software development projects?

- *Deviation*: Does this deviate from the core business?

- *Do ability*: How practical is this in real terms?

- *IP leakage*: Intellectual property can leak from third-party organizations.

- *Development practices/methodologies*

The process of software engineering, i.e., building and deploying software components to meet a set of business/system functional and nonfunctional requirements to support use cases, has greatly matured

over the past few decades. It is important that the
enterprise architect is aware of the various methods
and is promoting best practices for the method
adopted by their organization in relation to the build
and delivery of application capabilities.

Although these are well-documented elsewhere, we will briefly
mention two popular methods, i.e., the Waterfall and Agile methods.

Waterfall is a sequential process, in that each phase does not overlap
with a set of specific deliverables and review/gate processes built into
the cycle.

Waterfall follows a logical progression sequential phase within the
project lifecycle process (see Figure 6-4). Some of the key principles in
Waterfall include a sequential structure. This software development
lifecycle (SDLC) model allows the breakdown and demarcation of
activities, with "project" gates built in to ensure command and control of
all activities.

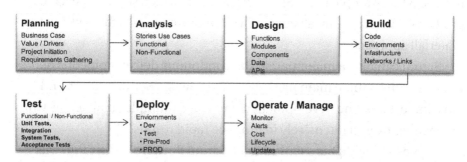

Figure 6-4. *Waterfall SDLC*

Planning does not appear on the EA radar, as it is very much a
project management activity. It is important, as it sparks the investment
constraints and project structures and deliverables.

The Analysis phase addresses both functional and non-functional needs, exploring options, to deliver a solution against these requirements. This is then followed by a design, build, test and deployment stage which drives realization of the solution into production. (This is discussed further in "Solution Architects - Chapter 14")

The authors of the *Agile software development* method state that it "is more than frameworks such as Scrum, Extreme Programming, or Feature-Driven Development (FDD)." It is important to note that the concepts are built on a set of processes where both requirements and the solution evolve through continuous collaborative cross-functional teams and end users.

Agile advocates an adaptive planning, evolutionary development with early delivery and continual improvement to encourage rapid and flexible responses to any changes.

There are many frameworks that support the Agile Manifesto [13] to illustrate this continuous development, while the end outcome is not fully defined. One example is the Scrum framework, which seeks to develop a product or service in the absence of a full requirements catalog like in the Waterfall approach.

Scrum can play a major part in the continuous delivery pipeline of projects with its three main parties: product owner, Scrum master, and most importantly the development team where multiple small teams work independently and intensively to produce rapid results.

Figure 6-5 highlights a typical Agile Scrum flow. It's a basic flow that includes the following elements and phases or products:

- *User stories*: There will often be multiple user stories within the overall idea that represent the natural language. They are informal descriptions of one or more features of a software system to support the idea. User stories should be written from the perspective of an end user or user of the system.

- *Product backlog*: This represents the list of all things that need to be undertaken to meet the user stories and deliver the new product or service. It is occasionally referred to as the *to-do list* and a key "artifact" within the Scrum software development framework.

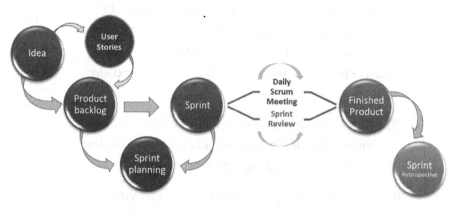

Figure 6-5. *The Agile/Scrum flow*

The backlog will be prioritized by the product owner, which is agreed on and then handed over to the sprint planning group.

- *Sprint planning*: This is the process where the team agrees to complete a set product backlog items from the uncommitted backlog to the sprint (i.e., stuff they will attempt to do from the master backlog list).

During planning, the duration, effort, and repeatability of the work cycle is clarified and "time boxed" with specific outcomes defined and distributed in relation to the team's capabilities and capacity.

- A *sprint* is commonly referred to as when one runs at full speed over a short distance, i.e., the execution of the goal; often there are many sprints to deliver the backlog items.

- *Daily Scrum meetings*: These occur during the sprint (usually one per day). At the end of the sprint, the team has a sprint review meeting, followed by a sprint retrospective meeting. This normally is comprised of a few team members to discuss progress and any problems encountered.

- *Sprint review*: This is a short (5 to 10 minutes) demonstration of the functionality developed by the team, showing explicit functionality.

Following the meetings, the Scrum master can update the burndown/up chart, which allows the tracking of progression, as each product backlog is delivered.

- *Finished product*: This is the delivered finished product backlog item and formal agreement by the team to move onto other activities.

- *Sprint retrospective*: This is a form of quick surgical autopsy; it's time for the team to reflect on how they're doing and find ways to improve the probe and inspect and adapt to build quality into the process.

We provided a quick tour of two popular software development lifecycles. In most cases, you will find the adoption of a mix of both structured and unstructured techniques used in response to the operational aspects, skills of team, and time to market for delivery.

However, with the time constraints to deliver value, software is often developed with the emphasis on producing a minimum viable product (MVP), which can be released to meet the generic outcomes and functionality enhanced as requirements are further expanded.

The Agile flow becomes a significant undertaking, and the emergence of supporting frameworks extend the concepts to develop enterprise-wide systems. One such framework is the Scaled Agile Framework (SAFe) [24], which extends several concepts to provide the tools and structure in the form of principles, practices, and competencies to achieve agility using Agile techniques.

- *Analytics/business intelligence*

Analytic and business intelligence (BI) applications are similar in nature as they seek to provide and deliver valuable insight into operational processes and performance and exploit similar patterns and components to deliver the results, e.g., the methods to ingest and aggregate data.

These types of applications collect, aggregate, analyze, and render information/metrics of value relating to real-time business performance and activities allowing dynamic recalibration or fine-tuning of their business processes to optimize the support for their BOM.

Analytic and monitoring tools provide a powerful set of utilities that enable immediate real-time calibration when a process, product, or capability is failing. BI tools allow for better planning and scheduling of activities.

Analytics tools leverage unstructured data objects, in the form of miscellaneous feeds (journals, images, files, emails, videos) from external sources or from internal persistent data stores facilitating the provision of intelligence, which can add value to the organization through visual representation and analysis.

BI tools are used extensively in business operations to aggregate and report information. Financial organizations, due to Anti Money laundering (AML) obligations, must gather and report on customers, which is known as *know your customer* (KYC) compliance checks. These checks can result in analyzing information from multiple sources such as the UN sanctions list of politically exposed individuals or credit-vetting agencies.

- *Inter-application connectivity*

Modern applications require the ability to exchange and interact with each other to share both data and functionality.

Applications, therefore, are not designed to operate in isolation or in a stand-alone manor with the exception of air-gapped[2] systems designed for security reasons, so it is important that these applications are designed to expose or consume services subject to a predefined set of rules for data exchange.

APIs are agreed upon functions that allow applications to access data and interact with external software

---

[2] An *air gap* system represents a security measure that separates a computer network physically, thus isolating it from unsecured networks, such as the Internet or an unsecured local area network.

components or micro services where the protocols, procedures, and tools that allow interaction between two applications are clearly defined.

Patterns for Integration have been well-documented, with a key recommended source being *Enterprise Integration Patterns by Hohpe/Woolf* (64 patterns) [14], where patterns for the exchange of information and the associated rules/structures to be established are shown to encapsulate the endpoints, message, channels, routing, translators, and monitors, as depicted in Figure 6-6, which highlights the path for message exchange.

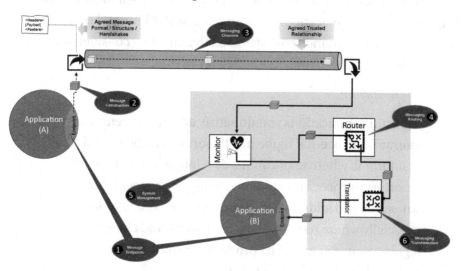

Figure 6-6. *Example focal points for an enterprise integration patterns*

Figure 6-6 depicts the key focal points for integrating or exchanging information between two systems where prior to any exchange two key factors need to be established and agreed upon.

- An agreement, between parties, on the format (syntax) and structure (payload). This agreement should also encapsulate the protocols for acceptance and rejection of any messages.

- It is also critical to agree on and establish a trust relationship between the parties, which would include the management of any security keys and the connection protocols to ensure that integrity of the message being sent/received is protected in transit.

Enterprise architects must manage the portfolio of interfaces, which allows information to travel in, out, and within their organization. This leads to complexity in terms of performance, scalability, and security resulting in a maintenance cost overhead that must be considered when building large federated and distributed services.

- *Reporting*

Reporting applications should satisfy all requirements for internal and external reporting. Reporting can be formal or informal, where applications developed or procured for reporting purposes are designed to factor changes in data structures and address real-time, dynamic configuration, especially where requirements are volatile and change regular. Hence, it would be prudent to avoid any hard-coding of reports where possible.

Some typical categories of reporting types or applications are as follows:

- *Operational* reports are often concerned with production-type data and provide information on aspects of the organization's day-to-day deliverables. Typically, they are short-term and structured around hourly, daily, weekly, and monthly data.

- *Compliance* reports present information to regulators and investors on the organization's obligations in obeying the applicable regulatory requirements and standards for the industry they operate in. To create compliance reports, data will be required to be gathered from multiple sources across the entire organization.

- *Dashboards* are a visual display of data and provide summary information on data sets, e.g., key performance indicators (KPIs).

- *Alert* reporting and notifications can feed into a dashboard or can be stand-alone reports. These types of reports are often used in real-time operational environments and list all the alerts matched against a set of predefined parameters or threshold for a given time.

Summary ⚙

The application layer is an important layer as it is at this layer that the capabilities required are "digitized" and delivered, which requires a complex set of skills not only in how applications are built but also in how they and the components are managed.

In this chapter, we highlighted basic considerations and deliberately excluded critical areas, such as version control and application rationalization. Still, we hope to have provided some insight into the core considerations, as summed up in Figure 6-7.

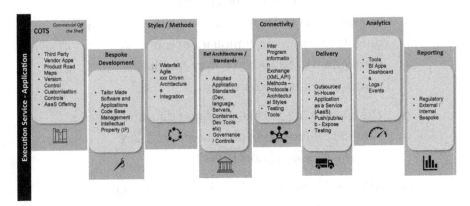

Figure 6-7. *The application layer and consideration summary*

CHAPTER 7

Layer 4: Data/ Information Services

The data and information services layer addresses activities associated with structuring, manipulating, controlling, and exposing data and information across the enterprise from a wide range of multiple structured[1] and unstructured sources. See Figure 7-1.

Figure 7-1. *Summary of data and information focal analysis elements*

Information, in most cases, is useful only when it adds value to a decision-making process, a business process, or a systems enabler. If information held in a store results in a change in a status, which triggers an event or an action, then this status change requires strict management and should have full traceability for reporting.

---

[1] Structured data is information that has a predefined data model/schema or is organized in a predefined manner to provide conformity.

© Daljit Roy Banger 2022
D. R. Banger, *Enterprise Systems Architecture*,
https://doi.org/10.1007/978-1-4842-8646-3_7

Data, when consolidated, transformed, organized, further processed, and then exposed as information to the layers above and below to support and trigger actions, should be both complete and consistent when exposed.

The nirvana is an information lake, which represents a 360-degree view of the enterprise (customers, third parties, operations, etc.). That data triggers/allows automated robotic processes to be executed, improving organizational efficiency and the customer experience.

To achieve these 360-degree views, organizations will adopt policies to build single authoritative sources of truth, supported with trust relationships, data integrity, and quality.

To support the concept of a single authoritative source of truth, data will go through a journey, where it enters in raw format and then transposes through various stages to something that has been validated for use.

The single authoritative data set or enterprise master data repository is best achieved through a journey enforcing stringent rules from the raw state to something cleansed and shaped to deliver value. In other words, value is constantly added as the data moves through its various stages into the single master data set.

Classification and Information Types

Before any information can be shared across the enterprise, agreements must be made on both its protection and access, i.e., who or what can view, update, delete, or amend data and how to enforce this with a trust relationship between all information-sharing parties.

This is partly addressed through adopting a data classification scheme where the data objects are classified when they are created or by assigning relevant categories (e.g., Top Secret, Secret, Commercial Confidential,

Internal Use Only, Not Classified) and then controlling how the data object within the categories are managed.

Information classification is not new and allows organizations to control "data buckets" during the data lifecycle, i.e., the repositories of data objects (information) used for specific purposes.

EAs and solution architects require an appreciation of the organizational data classification schemes. This awareness also demonstrates how the data is permitted to be handled, which becomes crucial to designing information systems. Therefore, data treatment and consumption policies often mirror use cases. For example, if the use case demands that the information should be for internal eyes only, e.g., real-time sales data or business unit performance data, then the classification of Confidential for internal use should be assigned. Any systems designed or built should enforce this classification rule.

The following are examples of data buckets that require controls to ensure regulatory compliance and avoid any threats to the BOM:

- People-related data can be customer, employee, or third-party lists, e.g., UN sanctions. This data should be protected in line with the relevant data privacy acts for the jurisdiction of operation.

- Reference data is very much static data; i.e., it does not change frequently. Examples are area codes and ZIP codes.

- Financial data can be transactional information. Examples are sales data or nontransactional data like budgets, general ledger codes, etc.

- Asset data is a subset of financial data, however managed in a different way, as physical assets may require additional tracking, monitoring, etc.

- Market-related data includes exchange rates, company share prices, etc.

- Systems data is information generated by the systems to perform their tasks, e.g., monitoring or alerting information.

- Banking includes all data relating to banking activity.

- Orchestrated data is data that is manipulated daily and includes multiple sources to modify the producing line or core business functions.

Enforcing controls and ensuring that the data is managed in accordance with the controls is discussed in more detail later in this chapter.

Enterprise Data Lifecycle/Journey

Irrespective of the source of data and the collection mechanisms employed, data will go through multiple stages before it can be used or considered of value to the enterprise. This journey, or sequence of stages, is referred to as the *data lifecycle* and represents a path where data moves from being just plain data to information, i.e., something that can be acted on by its consumers. This journey can be represented in many ways and can be broken down into multiple stages; however in its simplest form, it can be depicted as four stages, as shown in Figure 7-2.

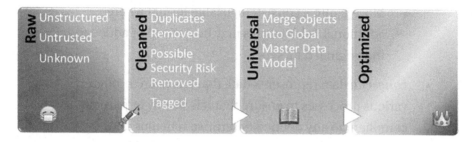

Figure 7-2. *Data/information lifecycle*

Figure 7-2 represents the transition from a raw to an optimized state.

- *Raw* data represents data not created by the
  organization at the source and enters the organization
  ecosystem through various channels sometimes in
  a structured (organized) form or in most cases in an
  unstructured format.

  In most cases, raw data is deposited into temporary
  staging areas to enable it to be quarantined before
  consumption by the enterprise. This staging area has
  two purposes. First, it acts as a single-entry point for
  data deposits, and second, it allows parsing for any
  potential security risks that could derive from the use
  of the data.

- *Cleaned* data represents data that is modified or
  adjusted to do the following:

  - Remove any duplicate entries to be found

  - Remove any third-party identifiers where
    appropriate

  - Remove any suspicious data items

- Move it into a consistent, usable format where additional fields or tags may be derived or added to the original data sets

- *Universal* data represents data that has been through various processes to ensure that it is wholly or partially compliant to any defined enterprise schemas and naming standards conventions implemented by the organization.

  In cases where the enterprise schema does not exist, then this phase represents the notional interim step where the organization seeks to reduce any data redundancy and improve data integrity i.e., the stages prior to optimization.

- *Optimized* data represents data that conforms to the group schema and provides the master data to support the enterprise. In real terms it has been "through the wash," and its integrity and quality are the best the organization can deliver subject to its constraints.

Tools are widely available to support movement of data between stages. These extract/transform/load (ETL) tools allow for data from one or more validated sources[2] to be pulled into a defined area (often a data staging area) and validated against a predefined set of rules for data ingestion.

During the transformation process, data is massaged to conform to any lifecycle rules. Rules should be then be enforced and further expanded with the transformation process and then loaded.

---

[2] *Validated sources* refers to the parties with a trust relationship in place and where the security protocols, IP addresses, ports, and passwords used to control or restrict the exchange of data have been agreed on between the parties.

When absorbing information into temporary staging areas, it is important to define and enforce trusted and untrusted data zones, as shown in Figure 7-3.

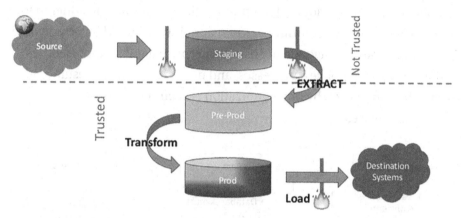

Figure 7-3. *ETL from source to destination*

It is important to ensure that the input/output into this "drop zone" staging area is protected/firewalled on both sides of the entry and exit route, which minimizes the risk associated with contamination from rogue data.

Enterprise Data Governance

Data governance refers to the mechanism for ensuring data is handled and managed effectively within the enterprise, supported by a set of processes and quality measures that can be applied to the data during its transition through the lifecycle considering the following:

- Agreed-upon data policies, processes, and control procedures, which collectively describe and enforce the data classification and management rules

- The elimination of any risks associated with poor data management both in terms of systems and processes

Data governance should where possible be a permanent structure within the enterprise, supported by a framework that sets out the roles and responsibilities related to data quality, usage, and accountability for compliance of any privacy and retention policies that must be adhered to.

A data governance committee, when appointed, should be responsible and drive forward the agenda to ensure enterprise data is supported by the appropriate polices, processes, and procedures, which result in data that when used by the organization is accurate, complete, and appropriate to use.

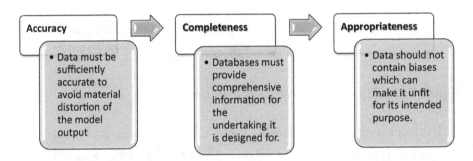

Figure 7-4. *Data governance goals: accuracy, completeness, and appropriateness*

The role of the data governance committee is multidimensional where at a minimum it should be accountable for the delivery and maintenance of the following:

- The corporate data model

- The associated enterprise data dictionary

- The semantics for enterprise queries, e.g., graph type semantics

- Key risk indicators and risk registers

- Control mechanisms and measures

- Data remediation work packages

- Compliance with all data privacy regulation interaction with regulator

- Data retention policies

- Responsibility for data custodians, i.e., the data owners responsible for ensuring that the data remains relevant; this can be a group or an individual responsible for the integrity of the data persisted within the organization

- Data ownership, i.e., the data custodians responsible for the use and rights to the data

We have discussed the main areas of the data layer, which should be considered as part of the EA work package to understand the drivers affecting the BOM. The data layer is an important layer, as this provides great value to the decision-making of the organization. However, there are three other areas that the ESA should be aware of and must have an appreciation of. These are covered next.

Big Data

Big Data refers to very large structured and unstructured data sets that when analyzed can provide information on patterns of behavior that can impact the BOM directly and indirectly. This refers to large data sets that can grow exponentially with time.

Big Data is data from several various sources and is often illustrated using the Vs of Big Data. The Vs are a great classification to derive more value from data and allow organizations to move toward a customer-centric path. Here are the core Vs:

- *Volume* refers to the quantity of data collected and is often measured in terabytes (TBs).

- *Velocity* refers to the data transfer rate with the target to achieve as close to real time as possible.

- *Variety*: This includes the types of different data, e.g., images, videos, and audio, collected.

- *Variability*: This includes data that arrives constantly from different sources and how efficiently it differentiates between noisy data or valuable data.

- *Veracity*: This refers to quality of the data.

- *Visualization*: This refers to the processes of presenting the data.

- *Value*: This is the key driver to achieve when transforming the tidal wave of data arriving digitally at the business.

Data Warehouses/Data Lakes

There are numerous products and supporting services that can be used to store large volumes of data.

Data warehouses are used to store structured, filtered data, which in most cases has been preprocessed and organized to conform to a specific schema for a specific purpose prior to its persistence in the warehouse.

A *data lake* represents vast pools of raw data, the purpose for which has not yet been defined, and the data is organized to deliver an "as and when needed" service.

By having data in a single area, organizations can easily analyze and investigate trends for patterns of behavior, enabling the ability to adjust its responses to these behaviors in favor of the enterprise or the desired outcome.

Before proceeding to the technology enablers, it is important to mention that for the enterprise data architect to drive and develop a single unified data model for the organization, they must be aware of all unstructured data within the organization. So, it becomes important that they provide strategies by following these core enablers:

- *Visualization*: How the data of the organization will be visualized and rendered to stakeholders

- *Connectors*: All instances of connectivity for static sources internal and external to the organization

- *Consolidators*: The points in the organization where data is consolidated

- *Ownership*: The custodian or individual or team responsible for ownership and more importantly the integrity of the data sets in question

Summary

The data layer is very much focused on the management and integrity of the organization information that is persisted and used. In this chapter, we introduced the basic concepts, terminology, and areas to consider.

Organizations use high volumes of data to make informed decisions on business activity, and it is crucial that the data lifecycle is controlled, managed, and supported by a solid information governance process.

CHAPTER 8

Layer 5: Technology Services (Logical)

Layer 5 represents the logical technology components and the groupings of physical technologies that deliver a specific capability to support the layers above and represent a set of *digital services* that provide executable system services. See Figure 8-1.

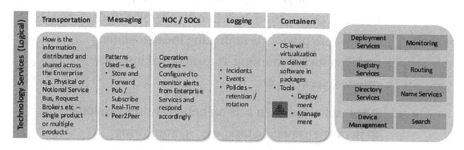

Figure 8-1. *Key considerations for layer 5*

As with all previous layers, this layer has multiple components, especially in a large technology estate, but we will touch only the core services at this layer that the architect should be familiar with.

Technology and services are in a constant state of flux, so the following list presents an overview of the type of services that should be considered at this layer:

- *Transportation* refers to the physical distribution of data/information around the organization, i.e., the channels and protocols, supported by various application products such as the following:

  - Enterprise Service Bus (ESB), aka the motorway for information exchange, represents a piece of middleware technology, supported by rules and principles, that enable applications to "plug in" or integrate themselves via the bus to receive/ share and expose both services and data between them and applications without knowing the details behind the connecting application.

  - *Brokers* promote application and service interoperability, acting as the translator/proxy between one or more independent applications or software platforms managing the associated services such as naming, transactional integrity, queries, security, etc.

  - *Agent* software often acts on behalf another system to perform a specific task; e.g., a monitoring agent may be deployed on server x, collecting metrics, taking actions, and transmitting them to application system y.

- *Enterprise messaging* has helped push the move to distributed/federated systems through support for the movement of data packets between users, systems, and third parties usually occurring in real time. Messaging can follow some well-documented patterns (see *Hohpe/Woolf Enterprise Integration Patterns* [14] for further information) but in essence adopts a broadcast or push/response approach.

- *Broadcasting* represents the distribution of a message from a source system to a single or group of recipients or target systems based on the target subscription profile for the message topic.

- *Direct messaging* represents a source system that publishes a message to a target system or a queue.[1]

- *Logging* is found in all organizations and as an enterprise service allows the recording of both system and user activity, providing the analysis and audit mechanism that delivers the ability to travel/roll back events that can then re-create or fix a specific problem that has occurred or even prevent this from happening.

Enterprise logging systems provide the user (usually service support functions) with resources to log information and to retrieve and analyze it offline later.

The following are the areas of logging that are important for the enterprise architect to consider:

- Applications logging for performance, usage, and errors notifications

- Technology environmental logging, i.e., event logging resulting from a change in the state of a device or system, e.g., failure

Enterprise architects will need to define any policies that relate to the retention of data and the policies for rotating the logs, i.e., deleting and starting again to ensure log files do not grow too large.

---

[1] Note the minor difference between a topic and queue in that all subscribers to a topic receive the same message when published, whereas only one subscriber to a queue receives a message when the message is sent.

- *Monitoring* sits, side by side, with logging in that it provides the surveillance and observational rules and subsequent actions to be taken. There are various types of monitoring that require the EA to be conversant in them.

  - Real-time monitoring is the ability to monitor events that happen in near real time.

  - Forward and parse monitoring is the process where logs are forwarded to a central hub or repository and parsed for error alerts and notifications are raised.

  - Agent monitoring includes the actions taken by a piece of software deployed to capture alerts or errors on behalf of a main program.

- *Containers* support operating system (OS) virtualization allowing multiple copies/instances of the operating system to be cloned and executed on the same physical hardware platform yet providing the separating to execute applications or micro services and discrete application in multiple versions of the OS.

- *Enterprise search* provides the software capabilities to perform a search for information across the enterprise. Irrespective in most cases of geolocation and data type, however, this is restricted to a limited search criterion.

  Search is a critical value business activity. The ability to locate information from multiple federated data sources is restricted only by the ability to plug and control the data sources often due to security restrictions imposed into the search software parameters.

- Routing, as the name implies, is the provision of the path or routes for the data between systems and applications to follow across an internal or external destination and networks.

- Name services map names or identifiers to their respective network resources or application services.

  Services are stored in a central place in the form of a directory where objects such as user, groups, applications, devices, and the associated access rights/privileges are bound and resolved.

- *Device management* refers to the management and administration of all pervasive devices consuming enterprise services.

  Mobile device management software enables management of devices, applications, and, in some cases, content deployed on the devices by applying security policies for the type of user.

Summary

Layer 5 is about the logical groupings of technologies and the resources provided by these groupings. This layer provides a level of abstraction that is required to segment the physical devices from the above layers.

Figure 8-1 highlighted the numerous key areas, and this area is a technical area that requires some understanding of the physical devices found in layer 6.

CHAPTER 9

Layer 6: Enabling Technology (Physical)

This layer represents the physical tangible technology assets along with the components in the organization that are used to deliver the enabling services and associated management and control policies. This layer is often referred to as the "tin and string" of the organization. See Figure 9-1.

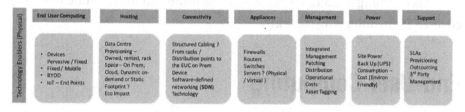

Figure 9-1. *Key considerations*

Computing hardware and the associated physical devices are no longer perceived as business differentiators providing competitive advantage. They have become commodity services requiring management and control, especially when the rate of change and emergence of new and improved devices for processing, storage, and connectivity are perpetually improving and becoming cheaper to procure.

EAs need to be aware of and constantly evaluating the "real value" offered to the business from these commodities and any associated costs and services.

© Daljit Roy Banger 2022
D. R. Banger, *Enterprise Systems Architecture,*
https://doi.org/10.1007/978-1-4842-8646-3_9

- The cost can be represented as either capital expenditure (CapEx) or operational expenditure (OpEx), which need to be managed and reduced over time, as they affect the profit and loss of the organization.

  Any costs associated with the technical debt, i.e., future possible costs (discussed in "Hygiene Services - Chapter 10") should be provisioned for where possible.

- Services refer to the provision of a full life-cycle management capability, i.e., the introduction of services, support, and general management through the life of the asset and the subsequent decommission, i.e., disposal of the asset.

This enabling technology layer, at a minimum, should include what's covered in the following sections.

End-User Computing

End-user computing (EUC) refers to a physical device and the associated capabilities of that device that support and enable workflow and collaboration with enterprise systems securely.

EUC devices can be fixed, pervasive, or Internet-enabled devices and systems, which provide different user experiences and abilities to leverage corporate systems.

Internet-enabled and pervasive devices require additional controls to ensure the integrity of the data and services being requested and consumed to ensure they remain safe when in use and pose no threat to other systems.

If the EUC device resides within the corporate network, it is relatively easy to provision and manage that device as it sits within a controlled trusted environment where devices are assigned organizational controlled network addresses or Internet Protocol (IP) addresses and the data transmitted from source and destination can be fully managed, monitored, and thus ultimately controlled.

Pervasive mobile devices (phones/tablets) require additional controls both in terms of the integrity of the data and services consumed but also in the management of the device. In other words, applications exposed to the user can be compromised over a single or multiple third-party untrusted network and require these additional controls.

Where the operating model requires data to be received from devices residing outside the boundary of the organization, e.g., Internet of Things (IoT) devices (consumer devices, digital-enabled animal tags or digital feeds from closed-circuit TVs), then it is important to ensure that the raw data being ingested via an unsecure/untrusted network is received from a known unique identifier/source address and validated upon receipt before any consolidation occurs.

Hosting (Physical/Virtual)

One of the biggest challenges facing many companies today is where to host its IT services. The choice is between hosting on its premises, where it has full physical control, or hosting in a third-party data center, which may or may not be shared with other parties.

The pros and cons for any hosting strategy extend beyond pure costs, which vary between organizations and should consider the following:

- *Costs*: Opportunity costs associated with the provision of the service including but not limited to the following:

  - The support of the hardware and connectivity between devices

  - Licenses for software consumed by the hardware

- Delivery of the service, i.e., patching and maintenance of devices

- The current investment in infrastructure and any switching costs

- In-house skills to meet the current and future demands

- Charge models for use of the services

- *Flexibility*: The ability to move its services is also a contributing factor as many third parties contractually will ask for an early termination fee or penalty for early redemption

- *Hardware elasticity/agility*: The ability to add or reduce compute power on demand subject to network limitations in terms of expanding the bandwidth for service delivery

- *Scalability*: The ability to scale the environment without performance or cost overheads, as the business grows or shrinks, i.e., the on-demand dynamics

- *Localization*: Organizations that operate in multiple locations having certain constrains, e.g., data that is geographically sensitive (government-sensitive data may not be to reside outside of the country)

Hosting poses a significant monetary and resource cost to any organization irrespective of the model adopted, i.e., a single or hybrid model.

- The data centers are wholly owned, with all resources (people, technology, and processes) controlled by the organization.

- The data centers are owned by a third party providing the physical building and the relevant physical security controls.

- Data center capabilities are provided by third parties in the form of one of three categories of cloud computing service mode.

    - *Infrastructure as a service* (IaaS) provides a complete wrapper around resources, data partitioning, scaling, security, backup, etc., on virtualized infrastructure (hypervisors or operating system containers) to deliver compute services without knowing the low-level details.

      In this service model, organizations do not need to manage infrastructure; it is up to the vendor to guarantee the contracted number of resources and the availability, resulting in a standardized way of acquiring computing capabilities on demand and over the net.

    - *Software as a service* (SaaS) provides an on-demand software distribution model where the licensing and distribution of the software are provided by subscription to a centrally hosted and managed code base by the vendor.

      SaaS alleviates organizations from the constant pressure of software maintenance, infrastructure management, network security, data availability, and all the other operational issues involved in keeping applications up and running.

- *Platform as a service* (*PaaS*) is the term used to describe the complete set of services that are provided, allowing the organization to develop, run, and manage applications without the complexity of building and maintaining the physical infrastructure.

  PaaS can be seen as midway between IaaS and SaaS. It offers access to a cloud-based environment in which organizations can configure, build, and deliver applications without the need to create long-term commitments, and costs can be more accurately forecasted.

Connectivity

Computer to service, device to network, information exchange with third parties are all examples of how computers and users require digital connectivity to function and are provisioned by both the networking and physical cabling.

- Networking allows a connection and interaction between nodes sharing resources on a single or federated communications backbone.

- Networks should be virtually segmented (address, subnets, etc.) where possible to enable the differentiation between trusted and untrusted zones to offer maximum protection to the organization.

- Cabling often does not factor into the work of many architects. However, building or campus cabling infrastructures should be known, especially if the building is owned by the organization and hence worthy of a brief mention.

Appliances

Appliances are devices or equipment designed to perform a specific processing task and provide the compute power required by the enterprise and can include the following:

- *Servers*: Providing the compute digital processing power

- *Switches/routers/load balancers*: Supporting the movement and sharing of data between the nodes on the network

- *Security devices*: Firewalls, probes, etc., which monitor (down to data packet level), assess, and protect all nodes within the internal network

- *Storage devices*: Tape robots

Energy

Although energy is a real commodity service, it is often overlooked by many technology functions because it's "just there." However, it must be noted that the consumption and management of energy require monitoring because it impacts the environmental footprint of the organization, which in many countries can be a taxable item. For example, environmental taxes raised £44.6 billion in the United Kingdom in 2014 [15] and thus can impact the BOM.

Support

All the previous items require support when things go wrong. Figure 9-2 highlights a typical support pattern found in most organizations, where the first point of call by the user or system is the support desk, which monitors, tickets, and assigns calls that cannot be fixed immediately remotely or by user actions to the downstream support parties.

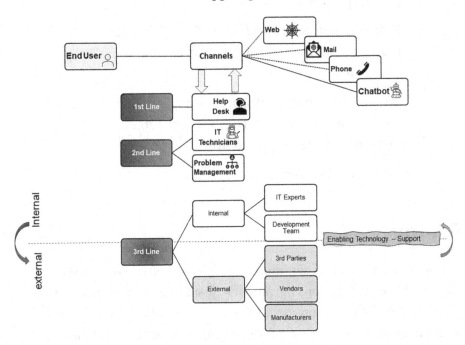

Figure 9-2. *Typical enterprise support pattern*

Management

The enabling technology and all the associated technology services require a structured approach to the management of not only systems development processes but also the operation of these systems. Several models exist for operations, which are mentioned briefly here:

- Classical operations (Ops)

- Development operations (DevOps), a concept in which the line between development and operations is blurred and members of each group assume some of the responsibilities of the other

- NoOps (no operations), a concept where the IT environment is fully automated and abstracted from the underlying infrastructure that there is no need for a dedicated team to support or manage the software

Summary ⚙

Layer 6 has two lenses, first the view of the physical enabling devices found in the technology ecosystem and requiring a deeper technical understanding of the devices used and the second lens being the capabilities and services these devices deliver and support.

In this chapter, we introduced the concepts of support and management, which in even a midsize organization can be mammoth tasks. That's why there is a need to structure and coordinate the service delivery, as highlighted in Figure 9-2.

CHAPTER 10

Layer 7: Value-Added Services and Hygiene Services

Value-adding services or hygiene services represent capabilities that are not essential but are more desirable, especially when the organization needs to maintain a steady state for the technology landscape.

Figure 10-1 summarizes the key considerations that should be encapsulated in any analysis and are discussed further in this chapter.

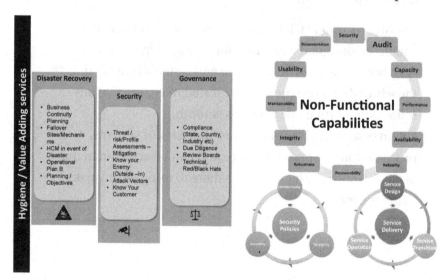

Figure 10-1. *Hygiene/VAS considerations*

© Daljit Roy Banger 2022
D. R. Banger, *Enterprise Systems Architecture*,
https://doi.org/10.1007/978-1-4842-8646-3_10

The following considerations need to be factored in when designing or building enterprise systems:

- *Nonfunctional requirements (NFRs)*

  NFRs represent operational runtime elements of a system, as opposed to specific behavioral requirements for the system required during its life.
  A complete sample of NFRs are listed and described in the appendix.

- *Disaster recovery*

  In the event of any business or system incident, procedures, processes, and backup systems need to be in place to ensure the organization can continue operating with a smooth transition with minimum disruption. Business continuity planning covers the full spectrum of planning, not only systems, but backup locations and the complete human capital management (HCM) of resources in a disaster situation.

  Disaster recovery (DR) with recovery objectives can and should be designed when building the systems. Relevant "run books" need to be designed and tested to ensure that the who, what, and when can be tested to ensure that any rollback to normal operations is smooth.
  DR, in essence, drives plan B, i.e., that a set of systems, processes, and tools are in place and can be acted on in the event of a surprise incident. It is there to mitigate any risks to the business.

- *Security*

Security aims to protect the business, including its physical and information assets encapsulating all the physical devices and enforcing the policies, practices, and standards for the organization.

Security involves a continual improvement process built around a wide set of tools and information security practices to monitor and enhance the security position of the organization.

Security unfortunately is not binary; digital threats to most organizations remain constant and ongoing. Therefore, security professionals refer to the security posture of an organization, where a good posture is defined when the core infrastructure is patched to the latest versions and in correct alignment and where all devices and associated policies are being used and enforced properly.

The following are some of the activities that ensure an adequate posture, i.e., where security policy addresses the potential threats and mitigates these through the following:

- *Threat analysis*: Reviewing potential digital threats to the organization and its systems.

- *Attack vector awareness*: The potential areas of attack. This analysis should also enable you to view the areas of improvement or hardening in existing systems.

- *Risk analysis (internal and external)*: Refers to the analysis of the threats and potential risks to the organization to ensure adequate measures are in place to mitigate potential risks.

- *User profile assessments*: To ensure the users have access to the appropriate information and data in relation to their roles and responsibilities.

- *Know your enemy (outside-in)*: Analysis of any potential external enemies, e.g., activist groups, state actors, and individuals.

This is an important topic for all EAs; in the following list, we briefly mention areas that must be addressed during the analysis of the technology landscape. However, we recommend Sherwood, Clark, and Lynas SABSA model for business-driven security for an in-depth approach.

- *Governance (see Part 3 for further information)*

  - Compliance and regulatory requirements (e.g., state, country, industry, etc.)

  - Due diligence and technical assurance for the systems

  - Review boards supporting the process of due diligence

  - Technical, red/black hats, deep dive forums

- *Security policies* that outline specific requirements, actions, and rules that must be followed when procuring, deploying, or designing a system

Policies are usually point-specific and will cover a single area. For example, "acceptable use," found in most organizations, is an example of a policy that covers rules and regulations for the appropriate use of the systems.

At a minimum, nonsecurity architects should be familiar with the CIA triad for information security policies (Figure 10-2).

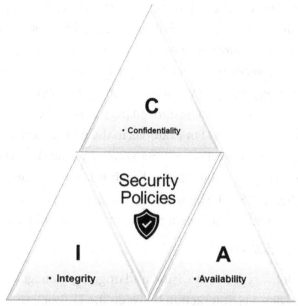

Figure 10-2. *The CIA triad for information security policies*

- *Confidentiality* relates to limiting and controlling access to information by authorized people or systems via security tools for access control and information encryption (at rest and in transit).

- *Integrity* is assurance that the information is both trustworthy and correct to its original purpose and delivered and received how the sender/author wanted it to be and not modified or corrupted in transit.

- *Availability* ensures that only authenticated individuals or systems have access to the reliable information and that countermeasures are in place to address any failure or denial of services.

No mention of the CIA triad would be complete with a comment about AAA, which stands for authentication, authorization, and audit. AAA is a set of primary models that aid in the understanding of the computer, network security, and access control. AAA is used to support the confidentiality, integrity, and availability security concepts.

In many cases, policies can be derived from existing regulatory requirements of the industry. For example, in the finance sector, it is important that the institution has a know your customer (KYC) policy that requires all new business to be validated against a set of precanned lists, e.g., the UN Watch list [16]. So, it would not be strange to see a policy saying "For all new business, validate the prospect against the relevant watch list."

- *Service delivery*

  Service delivery is the provision and ongoing management of the service, i.e., interaction between the IT function or service provider and its consumers/customers based on a set of predefined agreed criteria (e.g., service levels, performance indicators, etc.) agreed on by the function and the business. This is delivered through the following three phases:

  - *Design* is the activity associated with the analysis and design of all the elements (people, infrastructure, processes) to deliver the service. It follows industry best practices according to both the needs of customers and the competencies and capabilities of service providers.

  - *Transition* refers to the management of a technology estate where one manages both the deployment and any associated risks for the introduction and retirement of systems.

- *Operations* is the continuous fulfilment of user support requests, resolving service failures, fixing problems, and carrying out routine operational tasks to ensure that the service is delivered as per the agreement between parties.

For further information, please see the service delivery ITIL/ITSM documentation, which is publicly available from multiple sites.

The Stack: Additional Notes

In this part of the book, we introduced our stack. We did this to highlight the interdependent, layered nature of the components of the technology ecosystem. Each layer, while independent in its nature, consumes and produces services for the layer above and below to achieve the desired outcomes, which in essence is to support the organization in delivering its business operating model.

In each layer, we provided examples that demonstrate the interactions between layers to illustrate the breadth and depth of knowledge required by the enterprise architect.

The stack approach aims to help the enterprise architect align the technology landscape with the needs of the business from an operational and strategic viewpoint but more importantly develop the mindset required to manage the technology ecosystem.

On the surface, the level of knowledge required of the technology estate can be daunting; it must be emphasized that each layer will require a specialist architect to manage, as the level of detail required is immense, but segmenting the knowledge into layers enables an approach to achieving a macro view for the architect.

We have only skimmed some areas; for example, layer 5 is such a huge topic that it will require several different technical specialists to provide the required analysis and management. These roles are further discussed in Part 4.

Enterprise architects seek to map the layers in the stack, i.e., the business operating model and lines of business, to the enabling technologies to show synergies across business functions and technologies and in doing so can manage and control the technology landscape to provide cost-effective services to the organization.

This mapping allows architects to explore ways in which new systems can be built to reuse existing components across multiple lines of business and leverage efficiency gains in IT systems and thus reduce system touch and integration points.

Summary

Layer 7 is a "wrapper" service for all the layers and elements we have discussed. Security, disaster recovery, and service delivery should be baked into all high-level designs produced.

In the next chapter, we will discuss the typical products that support the mapping and governance to ensure that the estate is managed with the objectives of the enterprise architecture function.

Part 3

Building on the previous part, we explore some of the artifacts that support the stack, including how they can be used and grouped into either a CID, 5P, or both to ensure coverage and then clustered to ensure nothing is missed.

CHAPTER 11

Products for Delivering the EA

In this part of the book, we will discuss some of key products, or artifacts, that enable and support the delivery of an enterprise architecture (EA).

The term *artifact* represents an individual or group of deliverables or products that are produced by the EA function. This can include a wide range, from the delivery of a current state analysis, strategic road maps, support products, and governance products to that of the general views that aid the strategic, technical, financial decision-making of the organization.

Although difficult to quantify in real monetary terms, the benefits of enterprise architecture and the value associated with assigning resources to produce the various artifacts result in many benefits. These benefits can demonstrate value, and they can aid the control, inform, and direct (CID) artifacts of the management and direction of the technology estate to deliver and meet the needs of the BOM. They thus indirectly demonstrate value with a different lens.

- *Control* represents the formal, informal, direct, and indirect mechanisms in place to manage the technology estate.

© Daljit Roy Banger 2022
D. R. Banger, *Enterprise Systems Architecture*,
https://doi.org/10.1007/978-1-4842-8646-3_11

- *Inform* represents the artifacts that provide information to the organization, program, and projects to deliver the capabilities required to meet the operational and strategic goals.

- *Direct* is the actual path to delivery and the rules that must be followed to deliver the outcomes.

By dividing artifacts into CID segments, as shown in Figure 11-1, we can promote the prioritization to be performed. For example, the standards remain static and thus require less investment than, say, the update of funding models.

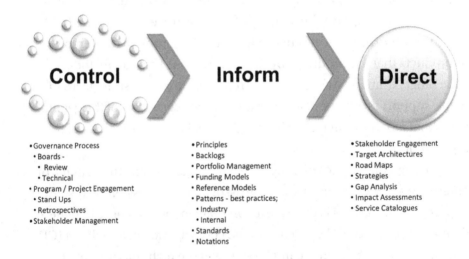

Figure 11-1. Control inform direct, artifacts

Before deep diving into the artifacts, it would be prudent to mention some drivers that can impose restrictions on producing EA artifacts and delivering the functional capability.

Contributing Factors

It is important to stress that the processes, deliverables, and artifacts from any enterprise architecture function are indirectly related to both the size and the funding allocated to the function.

All deliverables (breadth and depth) are subject to or directly influenced by one or more of the following:

- *Size and budget available to the team*

The budget for resources (people/tools) allocated to the EA function can either constrain or enhance the production of artifacts in relation to the complexity of the technology landscape.

Producing high-quality, relevant, and reusable artifacts is a time-consuming process and requires funding. In the absence of adequate provisioning, choices and priorities will be made to deliver the products and support processes to allow the team to manage the technology estate.

- *Organizational structure/size*

    One can argue that the size of the organization is linked to the size and complexity of the technology estate that is procured, operated, and managed, which in turn will impact the artifacts and processes required to manage the estate.

    In cases where the organization are federated across multiple geolocations with location specific regulatory rules and each location is thus acting as a separate entity in terms of data processing, this can result in a impact on the ability to move data across systems and deliver the benefits of the EA, i.e., reusable cost-efficient systems across the organization.

- *Characteristics of the organization*

  Management style and culture can easily affect
  the ability to produce and share artifacts across an
  organization. For example, in a military organization,
  where a "need-to-know" security policy is in force,
  information regarding systems and their capabilities
  will be restricted. This limits the ability to develop a
  single view of all system capabilities.

Figure 11-2 illustrates these contributing factors.

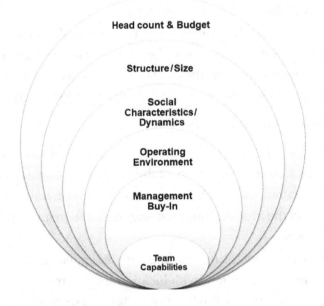

Figure 11-2. Contributing factors

Commercially dynamic businesses, with flat management structures
and short 'time to market' business models may not wish to invest in EA
activities, as priorities and resources will be focused on the delivery and
execution. These organization may also have limited skilled resource to
invest time on large enterprise type pieces of work e.g., building future

proof common shared platforms avoiding point in time solutions to address tactical problems.

Some organizations that adopt an Agile approach where tasks are divided into short phases of work with frequent assessment and adaptation so they can move quickly to deliver a minimum viable product for rapid use may not have appetite or funding to produce EA artifacts to support the enterprise as a whole or reuse of capabilities.

Organizations that steer away from a centrally hosted EA function and prefer to have operations in their respective markets, thus making a single unified view difficult to produce, restrict the provision of shared global functions.

- *Management buy-in of enterprise architecture*

   Because of the difficulty in presenting the value of EA in monetary terms, it is imperative that the management of the organization is committed to an EA capability. Where there is no management buy-in, there will be difficulties to raise funding, especially during times of budget tightening.

- *Team capabilities*

   The skill sets of the EA team and the understanding of the technology ecosystem will contribute to the delivery of an EA capability. See the Chapter 14 "Enterprise Architect" section in for an overview of the skills required for an enterprise architect.

This list highlighted variables that constrain the ability of an EA team to produce relevant artifacts. Figure 11-3 illustrates a high-level mapping between the stack discussed in Part 2 and the high-level artifacts irrespective of the size of the EA that can be produced to deliver value to support the BOM.

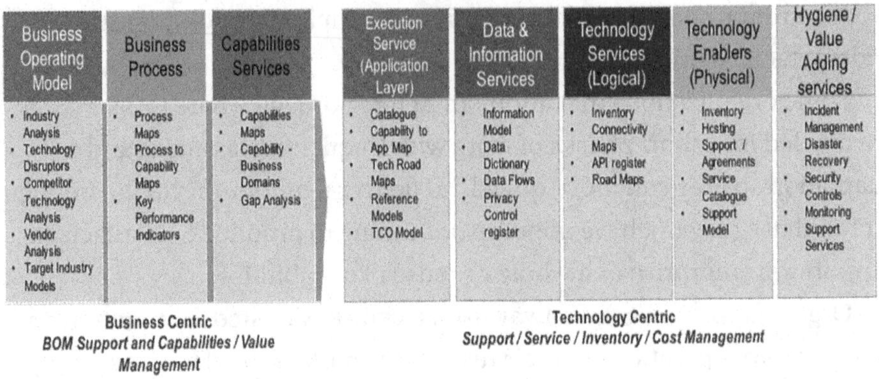

Business Operating Model	Business Process	Capabilities Services	Execution Service (Application Layer)	Data & Information Services	Technology Services (Logical)	Technology Enablers (Physical)	Hygiene / Value Adding services
• Industry Analysis • Technology Disruptors • Competitor Technology Analysis • Vendor Analysis • Target Industry Models	• Process Maps • Process to Capability Maps • Key Performance Indicators	• Capabilities Maps • Capability - Business Domains • Gap Analysis	• Catalogue • Capability to App Map • Tech Road Maps • Reference Models • TCO Model	• Information Model • Data Dictionary • Data Flows • Privacy Control register	• Inventory • Connectivity Maps • API register • Road Maps	• Inventory • Hosting Support / Agreements • Service Catalogue • Support Model	• Incident Management • Disaster Recovery • Security Controls • Monitoring • Support Services

Business Centric
BOM Support and Capabilities / Value Management

Technology Centric
Support / Service / Inventory / Cost Management

Figure 11-3. *High-level mapping of core artifacts to the EA stack*

Figure 11-3 highlights artifacts listed in relation to the stack. This view is a partial view and does not present a full picture, as there are additional processes and products that need to be produced to support the enterprise.

The following table illustrates an extended list and some of the most common enterprise systems artifacts produced during and as part of the ongoing delivery of enterprise architecture services.

The table lists example attributes and attempts to map, in terms of the artifacts control, inform, and direct, to the value presented to a business.

Name	Description/Purpose	Attribute Examples	C	I	D
Application program interface (API) management	The API refers to both the associated API artifacts, which could include structures and processes for managing the catalog, or the register of APIs encapsulating programming interfaces used by the organization for both public and private use.	• Name (public/private) • Endpoint (IP/port) • API gateway • Consumer systems • Message exchange protocols • Message payloads (e.g., JSON object format) • Security controls, certificates, ACLs, etc. • Systems exposed • Frequency • Service level agreement • Interface owner	Y	Y	Y
Governance: process	Standards, policies, and rules adopted to deliver and support the governance processes	• Process owners • Participants • Stakeholders • Frequency • Documentation links • Calendars	Y		Y

(continued)

Name	Description/Purpose	Attribute Examples	C	I	D

Application: component inventory, target architectures	Target state architectures mapped to capabilities for each of the platforms encapsulating all applications.
	Road maps for the application and portfolio.
		• Application inventories
		  • Name
		  • Components
		  • Support
		  • Versions
		  • Deployment info
		  • HLD, SD
		• Platform road maps
		• Capability to application maps that are color coded to highlight if we want to preserve, update, remove, or modify applications from the estate.
			Y	Y	

Architectural boards (review, technical, business board) with participation	The process to support the governance service and the mechanism of controls adopted by various support boards.	• Terms of reference • Criteria for evaluation • Calendars • Stakeholders • Waiver/exceptions Processes	Y	Y	
Architectural principles (system, process, generic)	Also known as guardrails; inform projects, architects, etc., about the principles to be adopted in the design, build, deployment, and management of information systems.	• Principles by domain • Guardrails • Patterns for use • Generic/specific • Publication	Y	Y	

(*continued*)

Name	Description/Purpose	Attribute Examples	C	I	D
Best practices research/ promotion/ socialization	Reuse and best practices for developing information systems; the channels for socialization and distribution.	• Reusable pattern catalog • Targeted channel distribution	Y	Y	Y
Business architecture target definition	Definition of a BOM and the underlying business capabilities, key value streams with the impacts of the drivers for change in terms of operations and cost.	• BOM/capabilities • Value streams/drivers • Capability models • Regulatory processes • Operational trend analysis • Process/workflows • Process to system mapping	Y	Y	Y
Data and information (MDM strategy), journey from data to insights	The data strategy and associated policies and standards to be adopted to meet the target direction.	• Information models • Custodian registry • Privacy impact assessments • Data lakes/warehouse structures/configurations • Data: inventories • Data: schematics • Data: information maps	Y	Y	Y

(continued)

Name	Description/Purpose	Attribute Examples	C	I	D
Financial/funding models (TCO, investment plans)	Budgets and cost models to illustrate key indicators, e.g., return on investment (ROI), total cost of ownership (TCO).	• Budget models/forecast for IT spend • TCO per platform/application • License costs • Service costs • Technical debt provisions	Y	Y	Y
Gap analysis (new solutions, transitional states)	When building new systems, it is important to understand the gaps that they are filling and any organizational shortfalls.	• Capability/service gap models • Roadmaps	Y	Y	Y
Group/system policies (sys admin, etc.)	The security-related policies to the directory and access structures of the organization.	• Directory structures • Access control lists attributes	Y	Y	Y
Impact assessments (projects, technologies, solutions)	Represent the impacts on the technology estate with the introduction of a new system or set of technologies.	• Assessment register/log • Risk register • Impact owner		Y	Y
Architectural risk register	Register or compilation of measures that are used to eliminate architectural risk identified as medium or high risk across the stack.	• Risk/source/nature • Options • Residual risk • Measure to improve • Owner		Y	Y

(continued)

Name	Description/Purpose	Attribute Examples	C	I	D
Infrastructure target architecture, enabling technology and platforms	Inventory of the Infrastructure used by the organization. This can be mapped to applications, services, or capabilities and to service level requirement.	• Inventory • Third-party support agreement maps • Platform incident management policies	Y	Y	Y
Reusable system patterns (dev, integration, etc.)	Pattern catalog to be used by all projects/programs delivering/developing new systems.	• Pattern catalog • Third-party patterns • Industry patterns (best practices)		Y	Y
Program/project engagement	This is the EA engagement model and the link to any project gate process.	• Terms of reference • Deliverables • Engagement model	Y	Y	Y
Reference models	These are the architectural reference models that are used by all architects for building and supporting information systems.	• Standards by domain/ platform • Models for each technical layer of the stack	Y	Y	Y
Technical/ application	Information regarding the technical aspects of the platforms in use including low-level details, e.g., operating systems versions/software, patches applied, etc.	• Technical inventory • Support models second/ third level • Disaster recovery processes	Y	Y	Y

(continued)

Name	Description/Purpose	Attribute Examples	C	I	D
Roadmaps (product/ technology)	A technical roadmap for all elements on the landscape broken down by product and owner and replacement plans.	• Road map • Replacement plans • Decommissioning plans	Y	Y	Y
Service catalog	This is the list of services provided to the organization.	• Services • Descriptions catalog • Spend authorization/ approvals • Service interfaces	Y	Y	Y
Strategy (product/ tech, deviation, etc.)	The strategy and substrategies for the platforms; discussed in Part 5 in more detail	See Part 5.	Y	Y	Y
Service promotion plans	These are the plans associated with service delivery and the route map from development to live.	• Service maps • Test strategy • Route to live documentation	Y	Y	Y
Stakeholder engagement	This is a process to supports the governance mechanisms and engages with relevant parties.	• Enterprise architecture engagement model	Y	Y	Y

(*continued*)

Name	Description/Purpose	Attribute Examples	C	I	D
Stakeholder management	This supports the previous process, but has a focus on management of stakeholders.	• Enterprise architecture communications plan		Y	
Standards/ notations	This is the notional standards adopted by the organization to visualize designs and process flows.	• Standards adopted/ training for process and systems modeling • BPMN • UML • ArchiMate		Y	Y

The previous table is presented for illustration purposes to provide a view of some of the artifacts that can or should be produced by the EA function to deliver and add value. However, it is important to mention that any artifacts produced should be proportionate to the organizational technology environment.

The table represents a list of artifacts providing a "supplementary addition" to the artifacts listed in Figure 11-3 providing a list to expand and produce additional artifacts that may be required or could be produced to add additional value, subject to the size and complexity of the technology landscape.

Traditional artifacts previously produced to support historic operating models may no longer be fit for purpose, especially when considering the adoption of new hosting models such as the following:

- The public cloud delivers infrastructure services made available to the public or a large industry group, owned by an organization selling cloud services, with responsibility for the management of the physical environment.

- A private hosting infrastructure operates solely for an organization either by the organization or by a third-party support organization responsible for the management, maintenance, and updating of the environments.

- A hybrid service represents a composition of two or more clouds (private, community, or public) using a service with orchestration between the platforms.

These hosting models will require artifacts that specifically focus on the agreements in place, not only regarding service levels but other contractual agreements, e.g., system monitoring policies. Thus, the artifacts will have more of a support bias.

Reference Models

Reference models aid the simplification, through visualization, of complex systems that when abstracted enable the understanding of system components and key architectural elements. This enables the provision of support and governance where compliance to a framework or reference architecture inures uniformity across the estate.

There are many excellent examples of reference architectures for both products and frameworks to build software. For example, the Java Jakarta EE Reference [11] (shown in Figure 11-4) presents a multitier applications framework that is supported by libraries and software at each layer.

- *Client-tier* components (applet/web container services) when executed on the client machine control the communication protocols, screen rendering, and any other elements that make the user experience consistent across all client platforms.

- *Web-tier* components (application client container) run on a Java EE server to handle the interaction between clients and the business tier and if required dynamically generate content in standard formats for the client.

- *Business-tier* components (EJB container) run on the Java EE server providing the enterprise business logic and micro services for the application.

- The *data tier* (although not directly shown) is encapsulated within the relevant containers and provides the data through the database management systems, keeping the data independent from the application services.

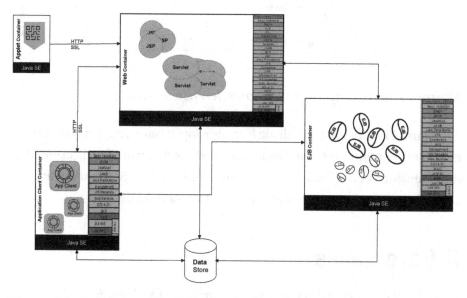

Figure 11-4. Jakarta EE architecture (source: https://jakarta.ee/)

There is no real standard for presenting a reference model, with notations varying depending on the architect or industry. However, application reference models tend to highlight key components, especially at the level 0 macro view for the process/service orchestrators and content, data, message flows, as depicted in Figure 11-5.

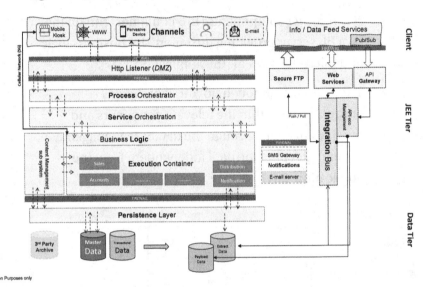

For Illustration Purposes only

Figure 11-5. *Example application reference model*

Figure 11-5 shows a simplistic business logic; however, this will have many components and many more interactions that would be presented in the extensions of the model. Each element in Figure 11-5 would be further expanded, dissected, and documented in the solution design.

IT Governance

We previously touched on governance when we talked about the data layer of the stack. In this section, we discuss some of the mechanisms and artifacts that aid the delivery of controls that help deliver compliant IT systems.

IT governance is a subset discipline of corporate governance and is there to provide the controls to ensure that enterprise IT systems, process, and reporting remain compliant with the regulatory and corporate standards of the organizations.

There are numerous frameworks to support governance, and not all are recent. Even in Tao, a philosophical tradition of Chinese origin, we observe writings on how a kingdom should be ruled. Methods, principles, and doctrines can easily be transposed and applied to the governance of a technology estate by encapsulating them within our standard policies, guidelines, and standards frameworks (Figure 11-6).

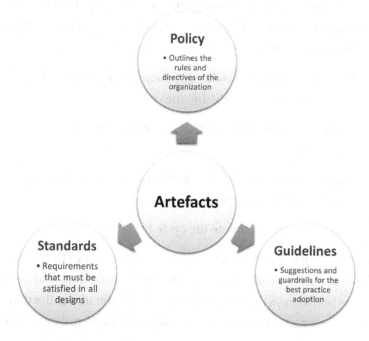

Figure 11-6. *Governance artifacts*

IT governance is often referred to as a *mechanism of control*, which wraps both business and technical behavioral rules around the drivers for any changes that are supported by standards, guidelines, and policies to ensure a consistent delivery of the desired technology and capability outcome.

IT governance does not have to be complex or costly but must be effective and involve all interested parties, i.e., the business stakeholders who define *what* is required and the IT function who define *how*. This will be realized and managed systematically to deal with all IT-related risks.

Regulatory compliance varies significantly by jurisdiction and can create operational challenges, especially when codifying the relevant rules on a group-wide level. In such a case, it is seen as prudent to adopt an industry-standard governance framework.

One of the leading industry-standard frameworks for effective IT governance is Control Objectives for Information and Related Technology (COBIT) [17], which aims to help organizations address the challenges in the areas of regulatory compliance, risk management, and the alignment of IT strategy to do the following:

- Provide stakeholders with direction to ensure that IT investments support the business

- Provide an effective way to manage and control any change

- Manage value from the IT landscape for the business by aligning with enterprise objectives

- Addresses the complete life cycle for IT investment

Although COBIT represents an industry standard for IT governance, it must be noted that the ultimate governance enforcement and incentive mechanisms will always funding and thus need to be under the control of the governance forums and where possible assigned to project gates and milestones.

Where standards are mandatory, i.e., dictated by legal requirements, the controls and reporting must be enforced indirectly by applying a systematic approach referred to as *compliance by design*, i.e., the integration of regulatory requirements, manual and automated tasks, and the relevant supporting processes designs.

The delivery of a smooth governance mechanism or processes is usually undertaken through multiple layers and often exposed via a set of design authorities, architectural review boards, program/project review boards, and product or functional committees, which are all responsible for ensuring that technology proposals align with the policies, standards, strategies, and road maps.

Governance artifacts can be derived from the organizational standards, policies, and guidelines that are adapted accordingly. Any deviations from these standards should be presented to boards with a remediation proposal, i.e., bringing the system back on track within a specified time and with the funding provisioned.

It goes without saying that the assigned governance and the delivery mechanisms, i.e., the boards that deliver the controls, must have complete management and senior stakeholder buy-in to ensure any decisions cannot be questioned later. This ensures decisions can be enforced with confidence. A board with insufficient authority will hinder the maturity of the EA within the organization and possible incur technical debt.

In the following sections, we discuss some of the boards found in many organizations.

Design Authorities/Architectural Review Boards

The architecture review board (ARB) and design authority (DA) aim to assess, review, manage, and escalate issues when required.

Design authorities tend to be closer aligned to a project or specific platform, while the review boards tend to focus on a corporate strategic direction.

Both boards, i.e., the ARB and the DA, should ultimately report or at a minimum be accountable to empowered senior stakeholders or subsequent management boards that act as both the parent governing body and escalation points for any issues that cannot be resolved at these local boards.

All ARB/DA actions should be managed and documented with any decisions reported to the senior stakeholders through various channels for full audit and traceability.

The chair of the DA/ARB will have a primary focus to address key technical issues and ensure at a minimum that one or all of the following is covered:

- Address technology and architecture issues that affect the organization's technology landscape, providing guidance and governance for programs, projects, and vendors.

- Ensure value to the organization is being delivered when following a specific technology path.

- Initiate reviews, when required, and recommend technology standards to be included into any enterprise architecture technical and target models.

- Promote reuse of system components across the enterprise and deliver both efficiency gains and cost savings.

- Escalate items, where appropriate, with alternatives and supporting information to allow stakeholders, as the formal judicators, to make informed decisions and minimize organizational risks.

- Act as the primary oversight body for IT technical decisions.

- Approve or reject project exception requests purely on technical merits.

- Facilitate architectural discussions and agreements.

- Escalate issues to the relevant committees.

- Contingency, if any, plans are required (for critical systems).

Governance as an enabling process requires several artifacts to be produced. These artifacts provide the audit trail for decisions and hence require formal minutes when making decisions.

Technical Debt Management

One of the key products or required deliverables from an EA function is the management of technology cost and current and future risk, both found in the domain of technical debt management.

A quick search with your favorite Internet browser will reveal that the common response for technology debt is "future downstream issues associated with the creation, maintenance and upgrade of systems that are either incomplete, have an untested code base, or have a poor customization and upgrade paths for software packages." However, little or no reference is made to other forms of technology debt, i.e., tight coupling of software components, connectivity paths, infrastructure, integration, or even the technical challenges associated with organizational mergers and acquisitions.

Technology debt, in essence, is the accumulation of the **intangible** ICT debt, associated with outstanding incomplete systems tasks such as testing, upgrades, bug fixes, patches, etc. In other words, it is the accumulation of all works requiring further completion or remediation during the life of a system.

If this debt is not provisioned for or repaid, it will continue to accumulate technical interest resulting in extra costs as and when functional requirements change, exposing the organization to a risk.

The easiest way to illustrate technical debt is to present two fictional examples. Both are on the opposite ends of the cost spectrum but highlight the implications of technical debt.

- An oil and gas company with operations across the globe and standard enterprise and SCADA[1] type systems require all maintenance records to be persisted (verified and stored digitally) and then made available due to strict regulatory requirements.

The delay in a version upgrade of their central document management system (DMS) by several years has resulted in software that is now out of vendor support. The DMS has been heavily customized to meet regional requirements and has several bespoke code developments and workarounds to accommodate legal requirements.

The supplier has now released a new product on a new architecture and no longer supports any versions less than two releases behind, resulting in a forced upgrade upon the organization if it wants to still use the platform. Unfortunately, ongoing customization of this COTS product and lack of upgrades has resulted in the accumulation of technical debt in the form of new software release or procurement, modification of the customized code to meet regional requirements, and the need for environments (test, dev, prod) and data to be migrated through the relevant environments. The resulting cost for this example could exceed $1.5 million due to the new software, the infrastructure, testing, and the much-required workarounds and bespoke code requirements.

---

[1] SCADA stands for Supervisory Control and Data Acquisition systems.

This example has a notional technical debt value assigned to it that has built up over the life of the platform.

- A solution provider with 6,500 users has neglected to upgrade its Microsoft Server software and the Intel hardware for several years. This has resulted in hardware that is no longer supported and only one year of support available for the software stack. The crown jewels of the organization are the user directories used by all systems; i.e. the Active Directory services are deployed on a Windows 2003 operating system (OS). The organization decides to redeploy (lift and shift) the software onto new resilient hardware, leaving the software as it is, with its one year of support left. Unfortunately, the new hardware does not support the 2003 operating system (hardware drivers not available, etc.). The choices available under such a scenario are as follows:

  - Take the financial hit and upgrade all components now.

  - Move to a Microsoft Azure cloud offering and decommission the on-premise internal hardware.

  - Adopt a virtualized 2012 server with 2003 virtualized containers, allowing for no further software upgrades for a year. This would fix the immediate problem but create "technical debt" because when Windows Server 2003 goes out of support, a full upgrade will be required. This leaves the company with a choice to take the hit or extend the technical debt.

In both examples, the supporting organization will incur costs to perform the remediation work; these costs form part of the provision for technical debt and will need to be met at some point in time.

Why Is Technical Debt Important to Enterprise Architects?

As previously mentioned, the management of technical debt is a core service of any EA function with accrued tech debt in the technology ecosystem of an organization compared to a tumor in the body, in that, unless managed and treated, the cells multiply in an abnormal, uncontrollable way and eventually affect the overall demise in the health and functionality of the body.

So, the question should not be *"Why is technical debt important?"* but "Should the organization absorb and avoid the financial cost now or live with the technology tumor and push the cost/effort to a future financial year?"

Unlike financial debt, technology debt has some unique variables, such as the skills time stamp, which lapse over time where programs written in COBOL on monolithic mainframe computers in the late 90s are still operational; however, the skills to maintain the code base is fast evaporating, as developers prefer to learn the latest object-oriented languages.

The skills time stamp is faced by many large financial institutions and utility companies with legacy systems built in the 80s and 90s now requiring an upgrade. We have seen in recent years many major transformation programs to re-engineer core systems costing millions of dollars to fix. One pattern observed is to build system wrappers around legacy systems to fix an immediate problem but still result in this overarching debt in the background.

Potential Factors for Technical Debt Creation

There are many factors that can contribute to the creation or inheritance of technical debt. Some of these are listed here:

- Incomplete business functional requirements.

- Lack of consideration for nonfunctional requirements.

- Incomplete code requiring refactoring, i.e., restructuring so that the internal code base meets the desired behavioral outcome.

- Hard-wired variables, e.g., static IP addresses in code resulting in software inflexibility.

- Poor documentation not only for production deployment but also at the design layer.

- Infrastructure; all hardware has a shelf life that must be managed.

- Poor enterprise architecture, e.g., the absence of enterprise master data management (MDM), which can result in silo-based data repositories with replicated information. This is inherited through nonstandard shadow IT systems delayed by business functions and not through the central IT function.

All these can add to possible technical debt; however, there are many other factors that may create technical debt, e.g., organizational mergers and acquisitions, which in most cases will create duplicated technology that after integration will result in some form of debt to either organization.

The goal of the enterprise architect must be to minimize, during the design stage, any impact and cost of future technology states.

Can You Avoid Technical Debt?

There are many ways to reduce technology risk; a primary example is at the enterprise level, where one should ensure that adopted products have **"road maps"** in which minor and major changes together with the underlying infrastructure costs supporting these systems is aligned to future portfolios and budgets.

When designing a system, the architect must ensure that the design considers factors beyond the life of the system and ensure best practices are adopted in the construction and deployment of the system.

Architectural governance, previously discussed, must be in place to ensure that the technology landscape is managed and that system best practices are followed both at the design and deployment stages, with any architectural waivers managed to align to a future technology state.

However, the dynamic nature of business often results in system requirements evolving, which means the underlying technology will always require enhancing, modification, or upgrade; hence, the answer is probably not. If the answer is no, then the focus must move to the management of this debt, as discussed next.

How Can You Manage (Repay) the Debt?

Taking control of technology debt has five key phases that are highlighted here:

- *Identification*: This is the hardest phase as this requires a detailed analysis of the technology estate and requires a detailed level of systems understanding.

- *Classification*: The method an organization adopts to classify the debt should align with the portfolio of project priority; a simple Red/Amber Green classification would not suffice.

- *Mitigation*: This should be run in parallel with phase 1 as the output of phase 1 should indicate initial mitigation tasks.

- *Fix*: This is the actual project tasks that define the steps to remediate the debt.

- *Manage*: This is the ongoing activities that should encapsulate all of the previous items.

Technology debt is an area that is often overlooked during the planning cycle and in many cases "creeps" up on IT departments without notice. Management of debt must be an ongoing activity within the enterprise and where possible contribute directly into the annual portfolio planning cycle, as shown in Figure 11-7.

Inherited debt must be managed, new debt must be avoided, and unknown debt should be provisioned for!

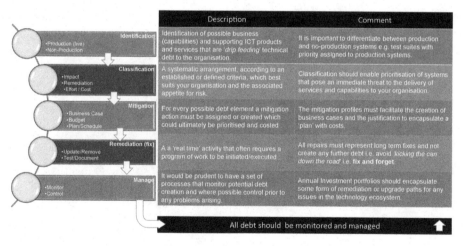

Figure 11-7. *Managing technical debt*

Summary

In this chapter, we introduced several topics that are required to deliver an EA capability in an organization.

We have listed many artifacts for illustrative purposes; however, it must be noted that these artifacts are not all be required to be produced to deliver an EA capability and are listed as a guardrail for you to use.

We discussed governance and technical debt management as they are related, and we provided the core concepts for you to consider in managing your technology ecosystem.

CHAPTER 12

Clustering Artifacts: The Five Ps Framework

In previous chapters, we touched on some of the core products and services provided by an EA function that aim to control, inform, and direct (CID) the strategic use of technology within the organization. To simplify the overall service provided by an EA function, we can cluster the offering into five distinct categories.

We refer to this categorization as the *five Ps*, which represent principles, practices, processes, patterns, and portfolio (Figure 12-1). The five Ps provide a simple framework to manage an EA practice and control activity.

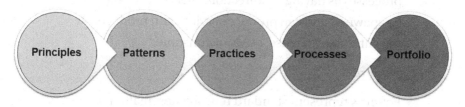

Figure 12-1. *The five Ps for EA enablement*

© Daljit Roy Banger 2022
D. R. Banger, *Enterprise Systems Architecture*,
https://doi.org/10.1007/978-1-4842-8646-3_12

On its own, each P represents a focus area or control mechanism that adds value, but alone it is not a true representation; when combined and consolidated, however, they can provide sufficient coverage for the capabilities delivered by an enterprise architecture practice.

The five Ps represent the following:

- *Principles*

  This represents a simple but powerful set of statements that promote, in most cases, a commonsense approach to selecting and building information systems with the aim of providing best practices to deliver and make technology choices.

  Although architectural principles are used for the design of capabilities, they are also used to force rules on the operation of systems and should form part of the governance process.

- *Processes*

  We previously discussed processes, the stack, and layer 2, and we defined them as a set of orchestrated flows or activities with a start and an end position that can be executed either in parallel or sequentially. We represent processes as having a bidirectional set of flows that can be spawned and can produce services and products for the enterprise to reuse, push, or consume.

- *Patterns*

  Patterns represent standard reusable templates for representations, components, and/or solutions to a common recurring problem. In software design, patterns aim to reduce the time to market for software components and avoid previously known mistakes.

- *Practices*

  Architectural practices represent accepted methods or systems-related activities one performs routinely, regardless of whether they are defined as formal policies or specified in each set of organizational procedures.

  Practices, adopted within the IT function, are usually based on customized methodologies that aid EA managers to constantly ask, "How efficiently has the organization adopted the practices and the approach, and are these meeting the business demands based on this adoption?"

- *Portfolio management*

  Portfolios are groupings of associated expertise that are classified, ranked, controlled, and managed by the relevant SME EA to control the needs of the organization (current and future). This consolidation approach of abstraction can and should occur in layers of the stack.

  Portfolios, as groupings, allow individual domain architecture experts to focus on their area of expertise. For example, the enterprise application architects can manage their "portfolios" and further decompose applicable criteria to ensure they are aware of all the changes that will affect the portfolio of applications.

The five Ps should not be seen as fixed; they provide a baseline or "starting point" to kick-start developing the products in an EA practice. This approach of segmentation enables the relevant artifacts to remain flexible to include other areas in the categorization; for example, you may want to create a new variable called People. While coverage is fundamental to the success of the delivery of value from an EA function, it is equally important to highlight that artifacts should be lightweight and adaptable.

Summary

The five Ps represent a simple categorization for the deliverables for an enterprise architecture practice/function and another checklist for activity. An example of a variety of artifacts, which when clustered or categorized to the five Ps approach, are provided in the example in the appendix.

CHAPTER 13

Managing Technology Change: Architectural Impact Assessment Guidelines

"Change is inevitable. Change is constant." This is a famous quote from Benjamin Disraeli, and it is true for most organizations. Organizations are dynamic in nature and constantly exposed to some form of change. This change is often driven by internal or external forces that ultimately push organizations to transform their operations, structures, or service offerings to address the opportunities and challenges arising from the change.

As highlighted in Figure 2-2 in Chapter 2, enterprise architects view the stack and associated systems from an "as-is" and "to-be" set of constructs. This view highlights a set of physical and logical objects that must be delivered to successfully move from the current state to the desired target. This transition, with its interim states, requires constant analysis to ensure that this can be achieved (the "do" ability) and that adequate resources are available and provisioned to address any required remediation steps and support the smooth transformation.

© Daljit Roy Banger 2022
D. R. Banger, *Enterprise Systems Architecture*,
https://doi.org/10.1007/978-1-4842-8646-3_13

173

In most cases, this transformation will impact the current operating model either directly or indirectly and subsequently impact any downstream technology systems and data flows. It would be prudent to undertake an assessment of any proposed changes to ensure that these impacts are both managed and provisioned for.

The systems used by organizations to run their business-as-usual activities (BAU) will have undergone rigorous testing and configuration before implementation and were designed to meet the specific functional and nonfunctional requirements. However, when a change is proposed or occurs that could result in a change to the characteristics of the runtime of these "stable" systems, then it is practical to revisit the original design and deployment models to establish if the systems will meet the new challenge.

Architectural impact assessments (AIAs) seek to capture and highlight the potential impact from a requested or proposed change, which could be a consequence of a change in strategic direction, business directive, or policy, which then modifies one or more system components, process orchestrations, or general workflows that deliver against the original requirements the system was designed for.

AIAs should not be confused with business impact assessments (BIAs), which establish the consequences of a disruption of a business function or process and consolidate information needed to develop recovery strategies for the business. BIAs start by defining the level of criticality of a system to the organization, which then drives the level of support and service required during the operational life of the system. Potential loss scenarios would be identified during a risk assessment, which should be mitigated against.

AIAs address the change with a systems lens and drive the decisions to provision the appropriate ICT resources that support the change and in essence identify the potential consequences of the change, encapsulating the cost and effort required to recalibrate any resources and components that are required.

The role of the architect is to analyze the characteristics of any proposed change and establish the breadth and depth of the impact, in relation to the system and or the technology ecosystem. Once the level and exposure of the impact are established, the next step is to establish the required components, effort, resources, and notional cost to address the change.

In the absence of a standard "playbook" for conducting the AIA, organizations will adopt methods that align to their technology stack and the associated vendor best practices. However, there are some common practices that ESAs adopt, starting with a cursory examination of any perceived impacts on organizational capabilities, services, or processes that could be modified because of the change that drives a variation in the business, technical, or operational aspects of the organization.

Figure 13-1 highlights a simple framework to structure and deliver the desired outcome from an AIA.

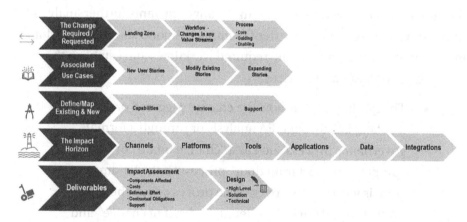

Figure 13-1. *Example architectural impact assessment framework*

Identify/Analyze the Change Required ⇆

The initial phase for an AIA is to determine if there is a case for further analysis, i.e., the "impact of the impact," and if it warrants further analysis and more resources.

The previous statement may sound a bit bizarre at first glance; however, one should observe that not all potential changes impact the technology ecosystem. For example, consider a new business directive such as "everyone should now wear a mask on site." Although this new policy/directive may impact the mode of operation, it will not affect the business model, i.e., how the business creates and delivers its value.

It is imperative that from the outset one establishes the type of change and any influence the change will have on or against the business operating model and supporting processes.

Once the initial assessment of the change has been undertaken, i.e., the cursory analysis to determine if the change warrants further analysis, the next step is to analyze the extent of impact. A good starting point, for further analysis, is to explore the required workflows and establish the required capabilities and services.

- The landing zone is how the change triggered or notified, i.e., through EA analysis or through a formal governance process such as a "change board" or "program/project front door" process. If the landing zone is via a formal governance process, then the project would have considered the "cost of change" and requested funding during the project initiation phase. If, however, this is not the case, then there may be a need to produce or conduct a business case assessment and trigger the relevant project activities to provision for funding.

- The workflow reviews encapsulate a cursory high,
  level 0 analysis of changes for flows of information and
  objects in an organization and hone in on the impact
  of the high-level business value streams[1] with the
  associated and linked processes.

- The process reviews will also include any associated
  orchestrations found wrapped around workflows and
  can be reviewed by exploring the following:

  - Core processes represent the enabling process
    and act as the foundation for all subsequent value-
    adding process blocks.

  - Guiding processes guide the evolution of
    workflows, i.e., the building blocks on the core
    processes.

  - Enabling provides the enablers and orchestrators
    for the multiple entities delivering the desired
    outcomes required by the workflows.

In this initial phase, we seek to determine and define, as enterprise
architects, if there is a material impact on our business and the current
operating model. If this analysis is positive, then the next step is to define
the functional and nonfunctional impacts, which we capture through use-
case scenarios.

---

[1] Value stream mapping is a lean technique to analyze, design, and manage the
flow of materials and information required to bring a product to a customer.

Use Cases

Having previously established that a need for change exists that will impact
the ecosystem, we proceed to the next layer of analysis and "dig deeper" to
establish scale. The approach of exploring specific business and technical
use cases includes identifying, simplifying, and organizing system
requirements, in other words, analyzing the functional and nonfunctional
elements of change.

- *Creating new user stories*: Here we explore if the change
  introduces a new set of business stories. For example,
  if the change is introduced by a new industry standard,
  how will this affect our mode of operation? This is
  best captured in a set of use cases or user stories that
  we map to people, processes, and technologies. For
  example, we can map the change to a customer journey
  and demonstrate the systems the new customer
  journeys will impact.

- *Modify existing stories*: If the change requires that the
  organization modifies existing functionality of the
  established system, then these requirements must
  be documented and captured, triggering projects or
  development effort. However, the analysis of the impact
  of the change will need to establish the cost and effort.

- *Extend/expand the current stories*: Enable existing
  functionality of the system to be reconfigured or
  enhanced, e.g., a new entity reported on a standard
  report that already exists but presents additional
  information. The impact may not be great in terms of
  systems coverage, but it will require clarification, effort,
  and cost to realize.

All these will need to be documented and assessed for impact and coverage capabilities, services, and support in terms of effort, costs, and overall change.

When moving from a current systems state to a new target state, it is important to understand the processes and orchestrations, which should be "frictionless" during the transition. Use cases and user journeys aid the process by highlighting to stakeholders the impact of the change.

Define a Map

Architectural impact assessments may result in triggers for new ways of working, new processes, and new systems that drive the delivery of the new desired business outcomes.

These new elements derived from the change should result in an update to existing architectural artifacts to reflect the mapping of these new elements to achieve the desired outcomes. These can be divided into three domains.

- The introduction of new capabilities, either technical or business, should be viewed and mapped against the existing set of capabilities to find any gaps. If the proposed change can exploit a capability that already exists, then it would be prudent to explore reuse to drive any cost savings. If the capability does not exist, then for the change to be permitted, the effort required to deliver this capability must be estimated.

  Services, either technical or business, required to drive and enable the capabilities to deliver the change should be analyzed. As with capabilities, the starting position is to explore what currently exists and map accordingly.

Services present the next level of granularity
and thus require additional effort for further
analysis. The delivery of business processes
should be updated to reflect the new changes and
the supporting tools, systems, and processes to
facilitate them.

- The introduction of a new requirement, i.e., a change,
will require analysis and recalibration of the support
architecture in many cases. The previous points may
impact the support components required to operate
the systems.

This list presents simple criteria to define a map of the proposed
change; however, the mapping at a minimum should consider the
following:

- User journeys

- Functional flows (systems/processes/orchestrations)

- Data/information flows

- Core technologies required to service requirements

- Support model; provision of customer, user, and
product services

The Impact Horizon: System Components
for Analysis

During the previous steps, we are in essence establishing the extent to
which the change will impact our ecosystem at a macro level and the
subsequent degree of change and the shortfall or gaps in our existing
capabilities and processes.

Next, we explore the impact on specific system platforms or
technologies, which requires a more detailed review to establish the
systems effort, costs, and importantly level of "technical debt" that may be
incurred during the introduction of the change.

During our AIA, we should look at individual systems and review the
following elements:

- *Channels*: These represent the entry point for
  consumers of the services and could be users or
  systems. Channels can be segmented into four
  domains.

  - *Digital*: Email, web chats, social media, interactive
    voice services, etc.

  - *Pervasive devices*: Mobile phones, tablets

  - *Online*: Desktop-based access via the Internet and
    extension of pervasive methods

  - *Direct access*: Branches

  Let us consider the merger of two companies, which
  offer identical products and services and adopt a
  new organizational name. Channel analysis during
  the AIA would scrutinize all customer-facing points
  and address the cost and effort of amending or
  refactoring these points.

- Platforms could be viewed as a single consolidated
  group of systems (applications, data, process
  containers, infrastructure, and other enablers)
  that deliver a complete service. The platform
  takes responsibility for delivering a single unified
  service, thus reducing new projects or other systems
  performing duplicate tasks. A good example of a
  platform is an organizational payment gateway that

181

provides a single entry/exit point for all payments the organization makes or receives and that provides the enhanced security required for payments and manages the integrity and confidentiality of all transactions parsed through the platform.

In our example of two companies merging to form a new organization, the AIA would focus analysis on redirecting payments and receipts through a single shared platform and assessing all downstream systems to make this happen with a view to simplification, cost, effort, and potential replacements.

- Tools provide the value-adding services that enable organizations to perform tasks and collaborate efficiently and can be used in any stage of the systems life cycle (analysis, design, build, test, deploy, or manage). Thus, any change to a capability service or process will impact the use of any tools or the way in which the information produced or shared in the tools may be used.

In our example of a company merging, the AIA can establish that common tools are used and that removing instances of duplicate tools would provide cost savings. However, the AIA should also highlight the simplification route.

- Applications are simply, as previously mentioned, computer programs that carry out specific tasks or group of functions to deliver a specific set of capabilities and services, other than one relating to the operation of the computer itself.

When conducting our AIA, we aim to map any proposed changes to a specific application or a group of applications in our technology landscape to establish the level of updates required or if a new system or amendment to an existing application is requested. There are numerous questions that should be asked, and they fall into two categories: Can we amend, extend, or enhance our existing application (physically or logically) to meet the challenge? Do we not have the capabilities and a new application is required? Numerous other questions can be asked, some of which are as follows:

- Can the proposed change be encapsulated in the existing application logic with some minor tweaks? For example, in our example where two companies merge, we may observe the volume of usage will increase, and the core functionality remains the same. This could be met by introducing additional hardware, i.e., simply add more system resources to the application to meet the increase in volumes.

- Can the change be accommodated by some minor configuration or application parameter changes? A good example is when an organization wants to report on a specific element and it amends its accounting ledgers with a new code specified and reported against its "chart of accounts."

- If we do not have the capabilities provisioned in any of our applications, how can we best meet the need: buy or build? The AIA should address the question with effort and notional costs presented.

- Data sits at the heart of all organizations; its value becomes evident when transposed and transformed into insights and information that drives and adds value. Hence, any changes, irrespective of size, may result in a requirement that may derive from the transformation of existing data sets or the ingestion of new data objects from new sources.

It is strongly recommended that the AIA initially concentrate on privacy and retention issue impacts and address the critical compliance to regulatory legal requirements, before exploring the types of data (structured, unstructured, and semistructured requirements) to deliver the desired outcomes proposed. The V dimensions of data, shown in Figure 13-2, can be used to further analyze the impacts.

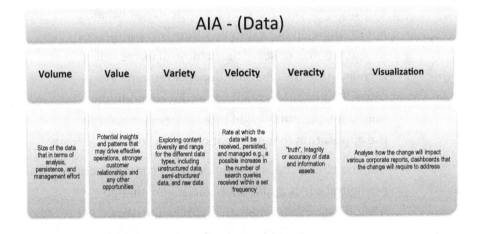

Figure 13-2. *V dimensions of data*

- Integrations require analysis during any AIA, as these
  are the vehicles for the exchange of information,
  both internally and externally to the organization.
  Integrations could encapsulate system-to-system
  information exchanges using application programming
  interfaces (APIs) based on agreed-upon standards used
  for the structure of data objects during the exchange
  of data. Any rework or refactoring would require
  substantial effort and resources.

Where data is shared via an API or a file transfers
mechanism e.g., Secure File Transfer Protocols
(sFTP) it should be assessed, especially if a
transformational process exists at the 'landing
zone' e.g., a process/script that is used to support
data movements between unsecure/untrusted
and secure enclaves. Any risks and gaps must be
identified and highlighted with a remediation plan
created.

It is recommended that the following, at a
minimum, as a pattern of analysis is undertaken:

- Message endpoints and the subscription services

- Channels, e.g., use of enterprise service bus
  or brokers

- The payload of exchange (structure and content of
  the messages exchanged)

- Any transformations, message enhancement,
  or molding

- Routing between source and destination systems

AIA Deliverables

The main architectural deliverable from an impact review is the AIA
document, which captures all findings and possible next steps. This
document can be used for a variety of purposes and more importantly
for different stakeholders. It is customary to find multiple mechanisms
of control for change in organizations providing a layer of due diligence,
governance, and gates to control the release of funds and associated
resources managing activity across the organization. Examples of such
mechanisms are steering committees, governance forums, change boards,
program or project boards, etc. Each one of these acts as the gate to
manage and control change.

Depending on the type and size of the organization, it is inevitable that
the AIA will be subject to scrutiny at various forums, acting as project gates
that control resource allocation, funding, and the authority to proceed. As
such, it will require documents to comply. But as a baseline, the architect
should gather the following information for presentation:

- A summary of findings, i.e., any weighting scores
  supported by charts to aid visualization of the problem
  and findings.

- A set of options and the likelihood that these options
  can meet the desired outcome. This should include a
  probability indicator that, if the event occurs, includes
  the consequences across the ecosystem.

- Technical components affected and the degree of
  coverage (physical and logical).

- The estimated effort required (structures, people/
  resources, internal/external).

- Consolidated potential costs to deliver the outcome.

- Impact on regulatory and any contractual obligations.

- The required process/system support modifications required.

- Referenced material (audit) such as high level designs, solution designs, and any low-level designs.

In most cases, the creation of a notional impact score HML (High, Medium, Low) together with a notional weighting that when aggregated ranks the options in relation to the scale of risk and degree of any impact should contribute to any associated artefacts.

When the change has been approved, then numerous architectural artifacts, i.e., the system design documents (used for audit), will require updating before the change proceeds. This in turn requires additional effort and architectural governance controls.

Putting It All Together

The previous discussion provided some insight into the purpose (i.e., the why) and a few guidance notes addressing the AIA (the what). Now let's consider a simple example that demonstrates how we develop the mindset to deliver an AIA (the how).

DRIVER FOR CHANGE

The government introduces an interim mandatory law. This law requires organizations employing more than ten employees to submit summary absence reports.

When the data is consolidated by health officials, it facilitates a feed into an advanced warning analytical system delivering in advance a view of potential pandemic-type outbreaks.

Reports must be submitted in digital form and in a standard predefined format to regional digital hubs.

To map the problem to the framework we discussed, we list some example architectural artifacts in the following table:

AIA Phase	The Context	Architectural Artifact Created/Impacted
Identify	New regulatory requirement, change required (Y/N).	Potential workflows and systems impacted.
User story	• As an employer, I must now flag any absences and immediately share the information with the regional government. • As an employee, I must notify my employer of the reason for the absence.	• Use case diagrams (UML) • Workflow diagrams (BPMN) • Notification service proposal • Modify existing channels, level 0 diagram demonstrating coverage • Capability matrix that highlights pottential reuse of components • Level 0 design and high-level design (HLD)

Mapping	• Impact analysis for the following:
	  • Data sources/flows
	  • Impacted systems
	  • Functional changes
	  • Digital channels
	  • Message formats
	  • Employee portals, HR systems (joiners, movers, leavers, JML)
	  • Time sheets/recording systems
		• Solution design document
		This document could take the input from the previous item and highlight the context to demonstrate how the impact will be addressed.

(continued)

AIA Phase	The Context	Architectural Artifact Created/Impacted
Impact	Review amendments and the exchange of all information between the various system domains and the endpoints. Note there may be some overlap with the previous review, but this represents a deeper dive. • Channels • Platforms • Tools • Data • Applications • Integrations • Security posture	• Platform, solution design (updates) • Low-level designs (new/ updates) • Security/risk reviews (new) • Level 0 flow (see Figures 4-1 and 4-3) • Service architecture (update)
Report	Presentation of findings and actions to the various gate and compliance forums. • Steering committees • Change boards • Architectural review boards • Project boards • Other control bodies • Any third parties (as required)	• Architectural impact assessment documents

In this instance, the driver for change is technology specific, and as such it would be prudent to create a level 0 diagram that demonstrates the impact and change against the set of existing technology services. An example level 0 diagram is presented in Figure 13-3, for illustration purposes, and this type of diagram should be created for the various governance forums.

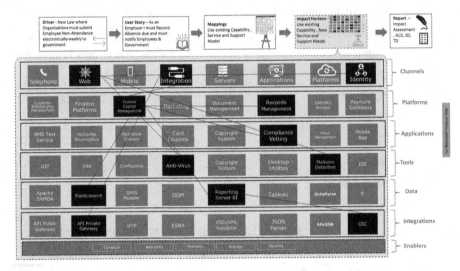

Figure 13-3. *Example of a technology-specific diagram with touchpoints and connections for information exchange*

Summary

In this chapter, we introduced the architectural impact assessments, which are a key deliverable for enterprise architects when any change is being considered or introduced.

In the absence of any standard approach, we presented a simple framework that one can adapt to meet individual needs.

Irrespective of any organizational approach, AIAs follow a simple pattern that we can use as a reusable framework for impact analysis.

Part 4

In this part, we cover the roles and responsibilities of EAs and discuss the skills required to deliver the artifacts discussed in the previous part, as well as the collaboration required by the architecture teams.

CHAPTER 14

Roles and Responsibilities

In Part 2, we introduced the stack and highlighted the associated artifacts that can aid in enterprise architecture delivery and support. At the same time, the stack helps develop the EA mindset. In this chapter, we will now explore the roles and responsibilities carried out daily by architects to deliver the EA services.

Architecture has always been synonymous with the design and construction of buildings. However, the IT community adopted the term *architect* to describe individuals whose primary objectives are centered on the design, build, and support of information systems.

This term *architect*, independent of the selected architectural framework the organization has adopted, is now used in many roles within IT departments, particularly those previously associated with subject-matter experts.

Architects, at a macro level, fall into one of three high-level categories, as depicted in Figure 14-1.

© Daljit Roy Banger 2022
D. R. Banger, *Enterprise Systems Architecture*,
https://doi.org/10.1007/978-1-4842-8646-3_14

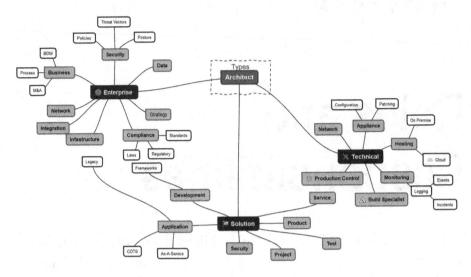

Figure 14-1. *Primary architect types*

The following are the core types:

- *Enterprise architects* are responsible for and maintain a macro viewpoint of the technology requirements and the capabilities servicing those requirements for the current and future operating models/states of the organization.

- *Solution architects* have a clear line of business program sight. They work on specific projects and programs and are responsible for the delivery of designs to support the requirements for the project and deliver its outcomes.

- *Technical architects* work on the technology enablers and deploy, manage, and support the services required for the business to operate.

There are many job titles out there, e.g., project, product, and functional architect, but in essence they will fall into one or more of the three categories listed earlier. Figure 14-1 extends some of the types for illustration, all of which can be mapped directly to a layer or group of layers in the stack, as illustrated in Figure 14-2.

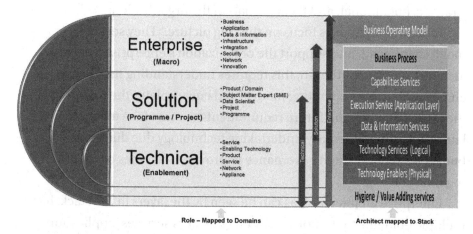

Figure 14-2. *Mapping architecture roles to the enterprise layered stack*

The systems architecture function or team can vary in complexity and skill sets; it may range from a single individual providing technology road maps, architectural governance, and general advice, to that of a large, multidisciplined group of individuals providing advice and products on a greater scale, possibly controlling and advising large IT budgets.

Enterprise Architects

As you have probably gathered, the role of an enterprise architect is a somewhat complex one. Enterprise architects must have both the technical skills to understand the technology landscape and the business acumen to capture, analyze, and understand the impact of any external business forces, drivers, and decisions (both strategic and tactical). These impacts must be understood in terms of both risk and gaps in the capabilities of the organization to deliver system solutions.

Enterprise architects maintain the organizational abstract view, with a primary objective to ensure that the technology landscape is aligned to the strategic, operational, and tactical goals of the organization.

Enterprise architects focus on the "big picture." They seek to mold, shape, lead, and support the organization's enterprise systems architecture. At a minimum, this requires understanding the current and target business operating models and encapsulates the mapping of the business needs and future requirements to that of the technology landscape, simultaneously undertaking technology due diligence, IT budget formulation, and governance to provide outcomes of value to the organization.

Enterprise architecture, as can be seen by the layers in the stack, has multiple domains to support, including business services, application, data, infrastructure, security, etc., which they must manage and address as part of their "business as usual" activities.

Enterprise architects seek to control, inform, and direct (CID) the macro-level technology decisions, working with programs and projects to produce, manage, promote, and, where possible, execute the technology roadmaps of the organization.

Enterprise architects, in essence, maintain the integrity of the technology ecosystem while ensuring that the systems meet the needs of the organization. To do this, they require a dual view of the organization, i.e., the internal and external views.

- The outward-looking view is very much reliant on the organizational challenges in the markets the business operates in and the strategies adopted by the organization to meet those challenges.

  To manage these views, we find that the architects structure their understanding by the organizational capabilities, products, and services all mapped to the value streams that deliver and add value to the organization. This is a very business-centric view.

This view is about the "business we are in."

- The inward-looking view, as one would expect, relates to the operational aspects and focuses on the processes, people, products, services, and technologies.

  Here the view is about "running the business."

  In short, the architect is very much about the value to deliver and consume (Figure 14-3).

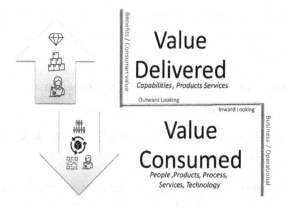

Figure 14-3. *Value delivered, value consumed*

Enterprise architects facilitate governance mechanisms by working with a wide group of stakeholders such as solution and technical architects, as well as projects and programs, to ensure that any deviations from reference models and previously defined target system states are managed.

Within the CID structure depicted earlier, the enterprise architect must ensure that any promoted outcomes can be realized and must ensure that cost-effective, tangible benefits and outcomes can be delivered to the organization.

Therefore, enterprise architects must have both the breadth and the depth of experience in the business strategy, as well as an understanding of the technology components in the landscape of the organization.

Enterprise architects must also be capable of maintaining a consistent, clear, strategic line of sight, while producing the various artifacts, including technology roadmaps, reference models, best-practice repositories, and technical standards.

Typical activities performed by the enterprise architect, while not exhaustive, can be summarized as follows:

- Provide strategic input into the technology roadmaps of the organization to shape, form, and stabilize where required.

- Influence decision-makers on technology investment, current and future.

- Provide systems consultancy, guidance, and assurance to large programs.

- Review and assure solution designs produced both internally and by third-party suppliers.

- Ensure that governance mechanisms such as review boards, principles, etc., are maintained and supported.

- Police the standards through project and program engagement.

- Represent the organization with third parties, for example systems integrators and standards bodies.

- Understand the impact of the introduction of new technology into the technology landscape of the organization.

Solution Architects[1]

The enterprise view is not one in the same as a solution view, in that the enterprise view encapsulates all the variables associated with the technology ecosystem and the "helicopter view," while the solution view is a single silo view of a specific solution that meets a specific need of the enterprise.

Solution architects are responsible for working with programs and projects to ensure a solution to a specific problem is designed, costed, procured, built, and delivered into the organizations, which often results in delivering a new process outcome and IT capability.

Solution architects address a wide spectrum of problems and issues ranging from the simple to the complex and thus require a wide range of skills (technical/business).

In most organizations, solution architects can be either generalist, i.e., have good all-round skills, or domain-specific, e.g., security, DR, infrastructure, data, networking, etc. However, both types of architects work with projects and programs to provide general systems consultancy services, such as impact assessments, end-to-end solution designs, cost models, etc. Products such security risk assessments, business/technology impact assessments, and solution designs are produced to provide a systems solution to a specific business need or to solve a current technology problem.

The work of the solution architect can be broken down into distinct project stages.

---

[1] Solution architects are focused on designing and delivering a complete solution to a specific business or operational problem. They may be given alternate titles such as project, domain, product, or functional architect.

- Identifying the problem

- Contextualizing the problem

- Eliciting the requirements

- Designing a high-level solution

- Estimating/costing the solution

- Working and supporting the route to live

- Transiting into service

Figure 14-4 illustrates these stages, and each layer of the solution architect lifecycle is briefly discussed. However, it must be noted that the focus at each layer will be aligned to the top layer, i.e., the problem/issue under consideration that ultimately supports the business operating model for the enterprise.

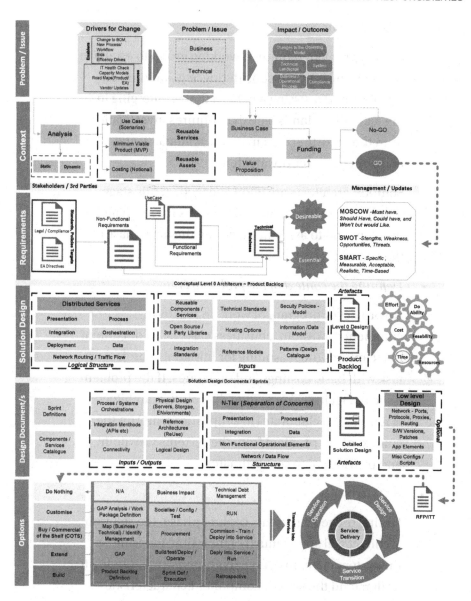

Figure 14-4. *The solution architecture activity flow*

- *Identification*

  Often a problem requires a working group to establish
  if something is worth considering, e.g., bidding on
  a project or discussing a pattern that is emerging in
  the technology landscape that requires investigation
  from the reporting systems such as capacity and
  performance/security incidents.

  Solution architects are often engaged, at this stage,
  to provide advice on possible options for resolving a
  problem and to assist in triggering the next phase of
  the activity.

- *Defining the context of the problem/issue*

  No project or program of work, in real terms,
  commences without a business case, i.e., a document
  that captures the reasoning for initiating a project or
  task with basic costings and outcomes. If the problem
  issue is a technical one, then the solution architect
  is required to elaborate (in simplistic terms) on the
  context of the problem from the systems viewpoint
  and provide some cost estimates.

- *Requirements*

  During the requirements capture phase, the solution
  architect will spend much of their time focusing on
  the system elements of the requirements and trying to
  understand the system component characteristics.

  During this stage, there will be a bias toward the
  nonfunctional elements of the system, especially
  as any assigned business analyst (BA) will focus on
  functional requirements.

One of the products delivered during the requirements phase would be that of a definition of a minimum viable product (MVP), i.e., the minimum components and effort that will be required to deliver the functional and nonfunctional elements and can be sketched to define further costs analysis.

The requirements must encapsulate any legal compliance issues such as the data privacy requirements and any additional enterprise architectural directives.

- *Defining product backlog and or level 0 systems architecture*

  Once the problem is known, documented, and decomposed into a set of clearly defined functional and nonfunctional requirements, a level 0 systems architecture can be produced to outline a solution.

  Where possible, all reusable components should be highlighted that will enable a shorter time to market and introduce any potential savings to the project.

  At this stage, the outcome should be a level 0 design and, in many cases, result in a product backlog, i.e., the list of objects that can be built to deliver for the solution.

  The level 0 design will facilitate the project to determine the cost and effort involved to deliver the outcome required.

- *Designing a solution with sprint deliverables*

  At this stage, a detailed analysis of level 0 is undertaken and elaborated on further to deliver a detailed solution design document and will include a list of technical sprints to deliver the project.

  Depending on the solution, it may be prudent to produce a low-level design to support the solution design.

- *Solution realization*

  We have previously discussed options available for analysis, ranging from "do nothing" to "build," but this should be further extrapolated to factor in both cost and "do" ability.

  The option selected must leverage existing relationships/services and deliver the best value for the money.

- *Delivering into production*

  Developing, procuring, or modifying a system that will be deployed into a production environment requires the ability to define these landing zones, and thus the solution architect must be capable of specifying the environments (test, staging, prod, pre-prod) required and especially the route to live through these environments.

  When delivering a system in production, the solution architect must work with service architects who will be accountable for the service and its operational elements (often extrapolated from the NFRs) of the system.

These needs and problems are captured at the analysis stage of the systems life cycle, during which both functional and nonfunctional requirements are documented. These are then used as baseline documents for designing solutions.

When considering possible designs, solution architects start by considering the following options:

- *Do nothing.* Leave all system components "as is" and perhaps just introduce new manual workflow processes that do not impact core system structures.

- *Extend* the existing system to deliver new functionality; this may be done by a partial new build, for example creating and then integrating new software components.

- *Customize* the existing system to work around the problem by a configuration change, such as adding an entry to the chart of accounts for a financial system to accommodate a new process.

- *Build* a new system to meet the needs. This option can involve the use of internal resources or external IT companies to the organization.

- *Buy* a commercial, off-the-shelf (COTs) product, which meets a minimum significant set of the requirements.

Solution architects work within the projects and programs to deliver the following architectural services:

- Manage the "cradle to grave," from conception through to delivery into production of solution architectures.

- Design both the physical and logical components of solution architectures that will deliver a positive business outcome.

- Work with project managers to provide provisional costs for the components of the architecture.

- Perform technical **analysis** and design capabilities.

- Capture business and technical requirements, when required.

- Facilitate design workshops.

- Validate designs/costs produced by third parties wanting to sell systems to the organization.

Technical Architects

Technical architects operate at the technical layer and work with the solution architects, production teams, service delivery team, testing team, security team, and others to ensure that the solution design can be realized and sustained in a production environment.

Technical architects will deliver additional designs at a lower level of design, based on high-level software and hardware components, and provide a more accurate cost built upon the figures provided by the solution architects.

The close alignment between the work of the solution and technical architect highlights the need for technical architect to be informed, sooner rather than later, and made aware of any solutions and technology choices to ensure that they can validate and mitigate any technical risks associated with new system entries into the estate.

Technical architects operate closer to the technology estate and are perceived as being more "hands on" and often aware of the real implications, in terms of cost and impact, of implementing a specific technology into the landscape.

Some of the typical activities performed by the technical architects can be summarized as follows:

- Delivering technical designs and standards and the associated approvals from the formal governance channels

- Awareness of the technology estate and the technology components of the organization

- Providing technical recommendations and options based on solution designs that can cost-effectively be realized in the production environment

- Mitigating any technical risks that could occur through the introduction of new technology into the landscape of the organization

- Providing input into the appropriate innovation funnels for the analysis of new technology

- Keeping abreast of technology trends and attending industry events to ensure product roadmaps are understood by the solution and enterprise architects

- Ensuring that production acceptance for projects is delivered and managed

- Performing impact assessments on selected technology

One can argue that the term *architect* is the simple rebranding of old technology-related jobs. This is true in part; however, as the complexity in the technology ecosystem has evolved, so has different "lines of sight" and the set of outcomes required of the roles.

Members of the architecture team must have domain-specific expertise, and they need to integrate with peers in the team, each having a degree of overlap and responsibility in terms of focus, views, objectives, and deliverables.

Enterprise architects will maintain the macro abstract organizational view, together with the understanding of the key business drivers and potential drivers for change and the effect that these drivers may have on the technology landscape of the organization.

Solution architects maintain a macro project view and deliver an end-to-end architecture in which they outline the key components (physical and logical) necessary to design a solution that meets requirements.

Technical architects maintain a micro view of the technical components that will be deployed to realize the solution design and often act as the true 'guardians' of the technology estate.

Architects will have different domains of expertise; for example, an enterprise application architect will be responsible for the management of the application layer of the enterprise architecture. This can involve managing the portfolio of applications and defining the best practice patterns, standards, and policies.

Aligning Architectural Skills to Competencies Models

We briefly discussed the roles of the enterprise, solution, and technical architects, which all require different sets of skills and competencies to perform the roles.

There are several skills and competencies frameworks that have been specially designed to provide a career path and some structure for progression within roles. These are mapped to an incremental functional competency.

A popular framework that is widely available is the Skills Framework for the Information Age (SFIA) [18], which describes itself as "a comprehensive set of descriptions of professional skills and generic attributes" and is used to provide an industry baseline for IT roles.

SFIA provides an excellent baseline for individuals who want to follow a route in terms of acquiring the relevant skills to perform a role. It also allows line managers and employers to understand the skill sets for roles and how to develop their employees.

Competency frameworks can also assist in developing pay scales to enable a structured mechanism of increment as the skill levels increase for the individual, and thus they contribute or add greater value to the architectural function.

Summary

In this chapter, we stepped back from the what and considered the who, i.e., the architect.

We focused our attention on the three macro architectural types that spawn the numerous specialist or functional architects.

We showed how enterprise architects focus on the macro picture, bridging any system silos in the organization and focusing on both the internal and external forces that shape the technology ecosystem.

When discussing the role of the solution architect, we introduced a typical flow diagram (Figure 14-5) that provides a guide for the work of the solution architect.

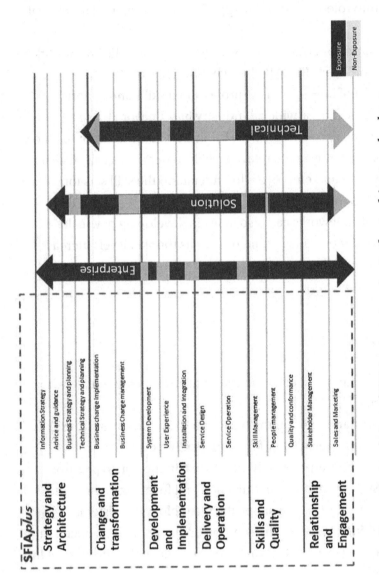

Figure 14-5. Example mapping of SFIA competencies to the architectural roles

Part 5

In this part, we consolidate all the topics covered and demonstrate the use of the tools to enhance the EA mindset. We also discuss the approach used to develop a key product of the EA function, i.e., the delivery of a technology strategy.

CHAPTER 15

Developing the ICT Strategy

Key deliverables for anyone working in enterprise architecture include roadmaps, investment plans, and strategies for delivering a technology capability to the business to support its current and future operational models.

There are many excellent books written on the topic of strategy, and in most cases they differentiate between strategy creation and strategy execution and focus on the business models and instruments that deliver significant change for good. However, these books to limit the information provided on the processes for creating a ICT Strategy which we will present below.

When considering how to deliver an information and communications technology (ICT) strategy, there are two approaches one can adopt.

- A *top-down/business-focused* approach with an emphasis on the economic model of the technology estate, i.e., costs and value-driven optimization of organizational resources that results in a set of cost-efficient capabilities to support the business in achieving its goals.

  This approach is closely aligned to the business strategy with a technology bias and attention to delivering business-supporting capabilities by constantly asking the question "How will the IT function deliver and at what cost?"

© Daljit Roy Banger 2022
D. R. Banger, *Enterprise Systems Architecture*,
https://doi.org/10.1007/978-1-4842-8646-3_15

- A *bottom-up/technology-focused* approach would focus its attention on the execution and supporting technology enablers and provide several "min-strategies" for each technology component. For example, this approach manages application programming interfaces (APIs) and how they are exposed to consumers.

  In essence, the strategy approach seeks to explain the choice of technology and the roadmaps associated with it.

In most cases, the strategy will be a mix of the two approaches. However, irrespective of the approach one adopts, it is important to consider the following:

- Understand the technology ecosystem in place, i.e., both the internal and external systems, their connections, and how they are used by the enterprise to meet its services and capabilities requirements.

- Appreciate if any ongoing technical debt is being accrued by the business. Often there are systems that provide and deliver current value, e.g., mainframe systems; however, as time goes by, the skills associated with the enhancement/maintenance of these systems vanish, and any future switching cost increases as does the accrual of technical debt, which must be presented in any ICT strategy.

- Understand the regulatory compliance required in your markets by the business, e.g., KYC.

- Understand the shadow IT systems developed by the business that are critical.

- Understand competitor/new market entrants and their use of technology.

- Be aware of the security posture of the organization.

- Understand disruptive market forces in the industry, i.e., any new or emerging technological trends.

- Understand mandatory controls, reporting and data retention policies, e.g., data privacy regulations for the jurisdictions the organization operates in.

- Understand cost models, internal costs, and any licensing costs for technology.

A Simple Strategy Pattern

To simplify the multiple approaches for developing and executing an ICT strategy, we introduce a simple pattern that illustrates at a macro level the processes and steps required to deliver an ICT strategy. A detailed example derived from the ING Group, using our pattern, is presented in the appendix. See Figure 15-1.

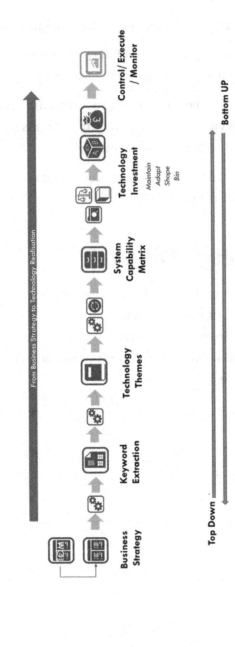

Figure 15-1. Simple reusable pattern for IT strategy development

Figure 15-1 highlights a simple pattern, detailed here:

- The *business strategy* represents the starting point where industry analysis has been conducted and the drivers to move forward for the organization are outlined.

    - The business strategy represents a main input for analysis and therefore sets the direction for the ICT strategy. It should consider the current and future operating models of the organization and, as mentioned, the important drivers for business change or transformation.

- *Keyword extraction,* as implied, extracts key words/terms, i.e., significant direction-setting terms and indicators that provide a default traceable baseline for the next phase.

- *Technology themes* represent the technology elements or bias captured directly or indirectly from the key word extraction phase, resulting in a list of themes that the strategy must support including other nonstated factors such as support technologies and any tech debt.

- A *systems capability matrix* is the matrix of all system capabilities required to meet the business strategy and any enablers required to support any operational requirements currently in place.

- *Technology investment* refers to the economics of delivery with reference to the existing technology estate and any new possible introductions.

- Maintain existing technology in use and the associated polices to "keep the lights on" and continue to use the technology.

- Adopt any new technology either to support a theme or to replace an existing product that is coming to end of life.

- Adapt technology to meet any new needs, e.g., upgrade versions.

- Bin or dispose of the technology that is no longer required; a good example would be the disposal of fax machines that are no longer used.

- *Control/execute and monitor* is the final stage, i.e., the management of the technology estate and any introductions of new technology. This section could also highlights performance and service indicators where possible.

This list represents a simple pattern to present the flow of steps required when developing an ICT strategy and adopts a top-down business-centric approach.

Note   The pattern represents the what but not the how, which encapsulates several other steps and additional sources of information.

The previous implies a simplistic set of activities; however, for clarity and appreciation of the enormity of the task, we provide an example in the appendix that is drawn from publicly available information for a large financial group.

The strategy cycles or flow of activities is further discussed next to provide insight onto the activities or process that must be followed when producing an ICT strategy.

The Strategy Cycle

Organizations annually capture resource plans to develop budgets that feed into their business plans. This internal approach to budgeting, short term in nature, tries to predict the spend by function. An example is "The marketing department will deliver x by spending y using z resources and channels." This can indirectly provide input and an informal approach to strategy development. However, this annual budgeting process is a very cost-centric approach.

This functional approach, while great for annual planning, provides a narrow reference for strategy development. Also, it illustrates one of many "levers" available to the organization to calibrate itself to deliver outcomes it may want to achieve over a period of time.

Levers represent the internal tools adopted to deliver a strategy and should be used where possible in the process. The process for strategy development and implementation must always consider levers, and with that in mind, it is worthy discussing the various phases during strategy development and execution, as presented in Figure 15-2.

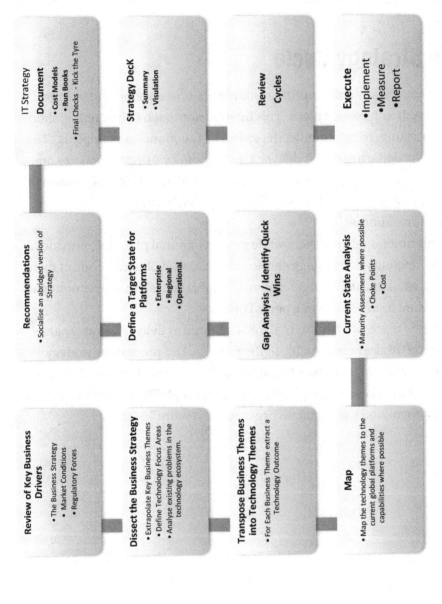

Figure 15-2. Phases for strategy development and execution

Figure 15-2 illustrates a typical strategy to execution workflow, where the following processes are undertaken:

- *Critical review of key business drivers* represents the business analysis of the operating environment and known drivers for change. This will result in a baseline for any subsequent work required. It is important to note that, now, one should consider the following at a minimum:

  - The current business strategy and any known drivers for change

  - Market conditions, both internal and external

  - Regulatory forces that require ongoing compliance and cannot be ignored, e.g., data privacy rules

  - Current IT budgets and spend to date

  - The digital footprint (social/API), which provides a view of the organizational interaction with the public that must be maintained or expanded

- *Dissection of business strategy* is a critical step, as this represents the breakdown of the existing business strategy, where we extract key business themes that we use to construct our wireframe IT strategy together with any perceived future and existing issues, e.g., areas requiring resources due to existing service issues, innovation, or general gaps or shortfalls in capabilities that would be performed through the following:

  - The extrapolation of key themes that we exploit as the high-level clusters enabling further technology segmentation. This approach also results in an audit map between the IT strategy and the business strategy.

221

- The definition of the technology areas, as previously mentioned, will start with analysis of the "as-is" technology estate and any strategic technologies that can add value to the organization moving forward. Technology areas must have a bias to delivering technology capabilities and not specific technology items.

- Analyze existing technology problems in the ecosystem including potential future (tech debt) issues that can and should be mitigated or provisioned for.

- *Transpose business themes into technology themes*

  For each business theme, a corresponding extrapolation is made in which the theme is mapped to a technology outcome, i.e., a business outcome to be orchestrated using a specific technology component.

  An example of a business theme is "We will respond instantaneously to fluctuations in the demand for spare parts." Here, one could extrapolate a technology theme as a need for real-time monitoring or alert notifications for minimum levels of sales orders. This will vary by organization, industry, and market.

- *The mapping activity*

  Mapping technology themes to existing IT platforms and their capabilities provides a view of the current capabilities available to the organization and provides a simple availability matrix, which can be further analyzed in terms of alignment with strategic technical objectives (e.g., simplification of the estate).

- *Current state analysis*

  This is a standard function for many architectural teams forming the foundation for their work in understanding the current estate and the issues with existing systems. This work will encapsulate the following analysis:

  - Compilation and maintenance of an inventory of the existing technology components, usually an extract from an existing configuration management database (CMDB)

  - The efficiency of the service delivery model currently in place, e.g., number of help-desk tickets raised and serviced daily

  - IT budgets/portfolio of projects, i.e., the pipeline of work, e.g., backlogs

  - Supplier both internal/external and vendor analysis (SWOT)

  - Although not always necessary, a formal exercise to assess the maturity of process, function, or capability allowing you to set a baseline that improvement can be planned

  - Evaluating any existing choke point, which is an area of technology that provides a bottleneck when supporting business processes

- *Gap analysis/identify quick wins*

  A gap analysis will emerge from the previous phases. The gaps are capabilities and systems that meet existing or future business operating needs. However, this should be documented separately where possible and act as a separate control document for change.

Some gaps can be immediately filled or fixed, with minimum investment, leveraging existing platforms and resources to deliver a minimum viable product that services these gaps and provides immediate value to the organization. This is often referred to as addressing the *low-hanging fruit*. Again, this is a priority issue to be presented to formal business governance forums.

- *Define a target state for platforms*

  During the previous processes, i.e., defining the IT "needs" in relation to the business operating model (current/future) and analyzing the existing technology estate and platforms, a picture will emerge of a target state landscape to aim for.

  This picture now requires additional effort to define the steps for delivery with resources and costs estimated and established to factor in the following at a minimum:

  - Procuring new IT systems or services to fill a gap

  - Extending the functionality of existing systems

  - Exposing the system functionality to new processes

  - Decommissioning systems no longer required

  - Removing duplicate systems of the estate

  - Any hygiene work, e.g., the security hardening weak platforms such as patching, etc.

All the previous should follow a formal review process, and thus they require documenting before moving onto the next step.

- *Recommendations*

    One would assume that any recommendations proposed should form part of the target state; however, this is not always the case and is ultimately considered a separate piece of work, with a slightly different target audience. In other words, core business stakeholders are less worried about the systems platforms and more concerned with the following:

    - The capabilities being delivered and what business operations they support

    - The investment required and the model of investment (CapEx/OpEx)

    - Resourcing (internal/external) required to meet the needs listed and the logistics around resources

    - Initial timelines for any delivery, subject to approvals and contracts being awarded

---

An abridged version of the strategy document should be produced and provided to key stakeholders for formal review with the detailed document to follow thus avoiding any complex future rewrites.

- *The IT strategy document*

Prior to commencing the production of the ICT strategy document, it would be prudent to agree on the table of contents with interested parties. This can reduce effort delivering content that may not be required.

A sample table of contents (TOC) is provided in the appendix of this book and has three main parts (illustrated in Figure 15-3), with three specific audiences.

Part 1 is targeted at senior management presenting them with a document summary focusing on the business-driven elements, e.g., revenue/expenditure/cost of technologies/technical debt, etc.

Part 2 is to show an appreciation of the business problems, priorities, and goals that the ICT should support and enable.

Part 3 should also address factors such as "keeping the lights on," i.e., the continual provision of service to meet the existing needs of the organization and any risks associated with using specific technologies.

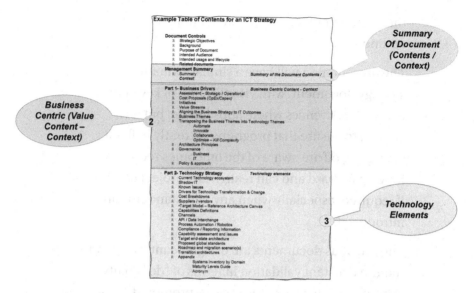

Figure 15-3. *The three-part ICT strategy TOC*

This is a living artifact, by which we mean that this should be updated when new information becomes available.

The effort in production should reflect the complexity of the technology estate and should be placed under version control and updated regularly.

The strategy in essence presents a budgeted plan of action, designed to achieve a specific outcome, and thus requires buy-in from senior management and stakeholders and individuals who will deliver the systems and desired outcomes.

The strategy deck (summary presentation) is another artifact that provides a "sales" type of spin/message to achieve "buy in" from the recipients and audience of the strategy, who may be responsible for delivering the strategic outcomes or system improvements outlined.

The presentation will have a similar structure to the strategy document, with visualization of key points, and with references where appropriate, but it is created to ensure that programs currently in flight or starting off are aware of the outcomes required moving forward and can realign any project choices if required, especially when any new standards are introduced.

The previous documents are of significant value and require constant validation in terms of "do" ability and overall integrity of the choices promoted. So, it would be prudent to ensure that formal review cycles are implemented and involve key stakeholders as well as the following:

- Midpoint reviews, i.e., reviews during the production of the strategy, ensure that variables have not changed.

- A content review is important as the integrity of the content should be validated with subject-matter experts when required.

- Internal approvals should be done prior to publication.

- *Implement*

  Extrapolating programs of work and subsequent projects will always be difficult as further analysis will be required to develop a business case in terms of detailed costs, milestones, and resource requirements, making the "ramp up" to deliver strategic outcomes a costly effort irrespective of project methodology chosen.

Quick wins as mentioned previously enable confidence to be developed and is an easy way to initiate strategic change that instills confidence in management moving forward.

With so many tools and books covering how to develop a strategy, we have only touched the surface of the topic. However, by introducing a generic pattern, we aim to help you develop the architectural mindset for when you are asked to contribute or develop an ICT strategy.

For an extended example of the approach, see the appendix in which we use the ING Banks business strategy to explore a possible path to delivering the contents of the strategy.

Summary

One of the key endeavors of enterprise architecture is the development or contribution to the ICT strategy of the organization.

In this chapter, we introduced a simple pattern that can be used as a starting point for strategy development and in essence provides a macro perspective for developing an ICT strategy.

We followed the pattern with the introduction of the *strategy cycle*, a set of steps to ensure that the strategy is not developed in isolation and any effort is organized, validated, and peer reviewed before release of the strategy.

This chapter emphasized how strategy and execution are connected, and both the pattern and cycle are related. We supported this with a sample table of contents for a ICT strategy in the appendix.

A Final Note

In this short book, we have attempted to introduce some experiences from the field, best practices, and guidance with a technical/commercial viewpoint in areas we felt would stimulate the architectural mindset. We also presented many diagrams to illustrate concepts and provide further areas to explore.

We provided a generic overview of enterprise architecture (EA), a term we use interchangeably with enterprise system architecture (ESA), where the emphasis is on ensuring that the technology landscape is providing value to the business and using the stack to allow mapping in a layered approach for traceability between the layers.

The layered approach, i.e., the stack, presents an overview of how the technology aligns to the business operating model (BOM) and highlights the elements required to develop the EA mindset.

IT viewed conceptually through a set of interconnected layers simplifies and forms the backbone of most business functions, especially where technology investments represent a growing percentage of corporate spending and when stakeholders expect investments to be aligned with business strategies.

EA products vary between architectural practices and organizations where they are often designed to fit a budget or align with the needs of the business used to control, inform, and direct the use of technology. To simplify artifacts, we can cluster into segments known as the *five Ps* to ensure minimum coverage is achieved.

The roles and responsibilities vary in the architecture communities, which have grown and evolved over the past decades. Technical and solution architects are the coal face enablers on projects and a conduit for

© Daljit Roy Banger 2022
D. R. Banger, *Enterprise Systems Architecture*,
https://doi.org/10.1007/978-1-4842-8646-3

delivering the enterprise architecture outcomes. By highlighting the roles, we hoped to show the close interconnectivity of them and some of the overlap in skills required.

Finally, we ended with the discussion with an approach for developing an ICT strategy that represents a major deliverable for most enterprise architects.

Throughout the book, we talked about the EA mindset, something that will help individuals to manage their IT ecosystem through promoting reusable enterprise patterns and artifacts and emphasizing the value derived by aligning the technology landscape to the current and future operating model of the business.

Appendix

Common Enterprise Architectural Principles

The Open Group has published a detailed set of enterprise architecture principles [19]. These should form the starting point for any enterprise architecture work. However, here we list some useful principles for illustration and explain how they can map to the stack presented in Part 2.

Applicable Layers	Principle	Context
0, 2–6	Strategic use of technology.	Technology defined as strategic should be chosen for all projects. Where current recommended technology does not support the capabilities required by the project, then a waiver/dispensation should be requested from the relevant governance body, and a request for technology standards should be revisited.
4–7	Standardization of technology (tools, processes, and systems).	Standards relating to the analysis, design, build, test, and use of technology should be adopted to deliver reuse value. Standards should be regularly visited to ensure they still meet the original objectives and provide the best value for money.

(continued)

© Daljit Roy Banger 2022
D. R. Banger, *Enterprise Systems Architecture*,
https://doi.org/10.1007/978-1-4842-8646-3

Applicable Layers	Principle	Context
8	Deviations from architecture direction should be managed and controlled.	Any deviation from EA standards should be controlled and managed through review boards and any possible creation of future technical debt minimized.
2–7	Simplification.	Technology choice should remain simple and where possible remove duplication for systems and processes that can be achieved by sharing common platforms with standardized integration patterns for information and data exchange.
2–3, 8	Design to reduce technical debt.	When designing, procuring, or commissioning systems, consideration should be given to future proofing the system.
4–7	Adopt, adapt, buy, build.	Adopt before adapt, adapt before buy, and build as a last resort subject to the organizational preference.
3, 4, 8	Design for zero service.	Systems should be designed to ensure that they require minimum operational supervision, and exceptions can trigger robotic processes to restore the state of the application.
8	Design for security.	Understand the threat posture/model for the organization and ensure that adequate measures can be designed into the system to ensure that all risks are mitigated. Security should be "baked into" all areas of the system design and product backlog.

(continued)

Applicable Layers	Principle	Context
2, 3, 8	Design for reuse.	When building a system, it should be capable of reuse both at the system and component levels; this reduces the cost of redevelopment of components.
2, 5–7	Design for automation.	Where possible, systems should be designed and introduced into the ecosystem with little dependence on manual intervention during its operation or runtime.
8	Design for self-service.	Where possible, enterprise systems should be configurable by the user to meet the individual requirements, e.g., setting screen colors, text/font sizes and subscription preferences, etc.
5	Data as an asset.	Data should be considered an asset, especially as it provides insight into the business operations and service demands, so it should be treated and managed accordingly.
3–4	Packages are black boxes.	Software and process packages should be treated as black boxes, where internal workings are not published to users or developers, and simply a request is sent to the package, some work is conducted, and the response is fed back to the user without awareness of the work performed to get the result.

(continued)

Applicable Layers	Principle	Context
8	Governance of non-IT-delivered solutions.	Governance should encapsulate all technology domains, and when the technology is introduced by business stakeholders, it should touch the governance process.
2, 8	Design for compliance.	To avoid constant checking, any systems should be designed to enforce regulatory and internal compliance standards.
2, 3, 8	Customer centric.	Where solutions and services are designed and built to ensure that any analysis or alerts do not distrust the customer journey and alerts to the investigator or agent are transparent.
8	Control the technology landscape.	Control is effectively managed through the government forums; however, there are informal mechanisms that require implementing to ensure that technology is controlled.

Task If you want, as an exercise, why not expand the previous list of principles and then assign them to the stack? Start with separation of concerns, which is a good principle to adopt but not mentioned in the list.

Business Models Definition

The business model canvas is a popular management tool that enables simple collaboration, visualization and the assessment of concepts and ideas on a single page by aiding the development of a business plan and strategy with its nine boxes that represent different fundamental elements of a business.

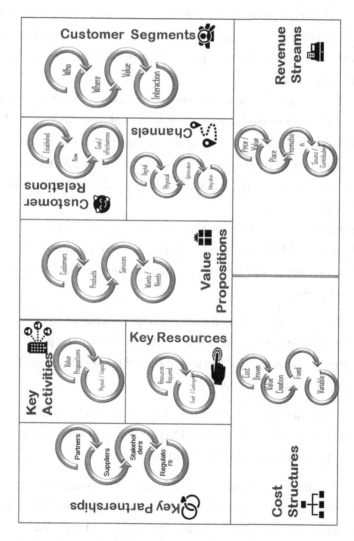

Figure A-1. *Business model canvas example (see [20])*

Example Industry Disruption: Regulation (PSD-2 Payments) and the Stack

Using the stack as a foundation, an ESA can structure a variety of control, inform, and direct activities/artifacts, discussed in Chapter 11. Hence, it is imperative to understand and consider the "what if" scenarios that may present themselves from any subsequent change. In this section, we highlight how a regulatory change can be viewed and mapped against the stack to provide a cursory view of possible impact on the organizational technology ecosystem.

If you inspect, work, or analyze the financial sector in 2022, you may have observed an increased level of technological transformational activity. This has been driven principally by new legislation, technology evolution, adoption of new business models, and the entry of small lean technology companies, which seek to directly challenge the established banking goliaths.

The emergence of new channels and technologies and the introduction of new European legislation has, to some extent, created a perfect storm for innovation and disruption in the payments industry with two visible explosions.

- The development of distributed digital ledger technology resulting in the creation of new enterprise models/markets for the use of digital currencies despite technical immaturity

- Legislation such as the EU European Payment Services Directive (EU) 2015/2366 (PSD-2) that is driving agility in the electronic payment industry

Currently, ample material is available online regarding blockchain, crypto, and digital currencies, which we cannot do justice in this short example. Hence, our focus will be on two aspects of the PSD-2 and representing the impact against the stack introduced in Chapter 2.

PSD-2 is having major impact on established companies operating in the financial sector, with the intent to further secure payments and drive the unification of transactions via the elevation of application program interfaces (APIs) supported by the "open banking" initiative where there is a focus on securely exchanging data by connecting banks, third parties, and technical providers under one technical ecosystem.

This "openness" and standardization has resulted in the upsurge of financial technology (FinTech) companies, which are slowly denting existing industry giants. Previously, for example, credit card companies controlled consumer payment models deriving income from three things: interest, annual fees charged to cardholders, and the transaction fees paid by merchant businesses that accepted credit cards.

Credit/debit card transaction fees have always been a bone of contention, especially with smaller traders who deal in high-volume, small-value transactions and are subject to a percent of the sales. A model with clear entry barriers (card devices, networks, etc.) is now under threat with the PSD-2 and subsequent use of the Internet.

At the heart of the new model is the important concept of "trust and consent," which must be given, obtained, revoked, validated, and time stamped for the new models to work.

A payment initiation service provider (PISP) lets a customer pay companies directly from their bank account rather than using a debit or credit card. This works through a third party by adopting the following simplistic workflow:

1. The customer provides consent to authorize the PISP to transact using a designated bank account with their bank where the authority is registered as active.

2. The customer initiates a purchase through a digital channel, which accepts the payment method via the PISP.

3. The merchant accepts the method of payment.

4. The transaction is transferred to the PISP for payment.

5. PISP makes an API call to the customer bank to check available funds and request a funds transfer.

6. There is confirmation of funds and payment initiation sent to merchant.

7. The bank validates and releases funds to the merchant bank.

8. The merchant's bank account is updated to reflect the credit.

Figure A-2 depicts this workflow.

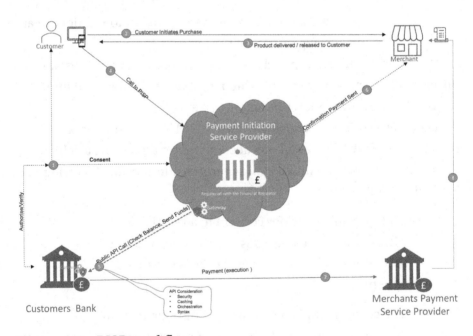

Figure A-2. *PISP workflow*

As shown, a PISP is a service provider that can execute a payment transaction on behalf of a customer; i.e., they can withdraw money directly from an account if they have the customer's consent. If the customer has more than one bank account, they can choose which account the funds will be withdrawn from.

Only companies that are authorized by the industry regulator can use open banking APIs to access financial information or initiate payments on behalf of a customer. In Ireland, the Central Bank of Ireland regulates open banking. Other countries have different regulators. In the United Kingdom, the Financial Conduct Authority maintains a register of account information and payment initiation service providers (see `https://www.fca.org.uk` as an example).

Another disruptor under the PSD-2 are the services provided by account information service provider (AISP). This is a set of services developed and offered by FinTech operators in the market that let customers/subscribers view all payment account information from different bank accounts, subject to consent, in one place online or via a mobile app and can analyze your spending.

AISPs can include budgeting apps and price comparison websites that offer budgeting help and product recommendations, which is a simpler model as no account changes are authorized.

AISPs act as "authorized" information aggregators and cannot transact or amend account balances held at the customer's bank.

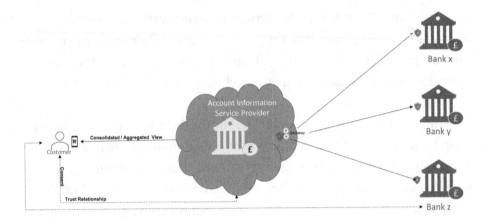

Figure A-3. *The AISP model*

Analysis Areas Mapped to the Stack

When considering changes to the business operating model, and in the previous case the PSD-2 impact on the financial sector, we start by considering the obvious elements on the stack that may be introduced or change to support the model. See Figure A-4.

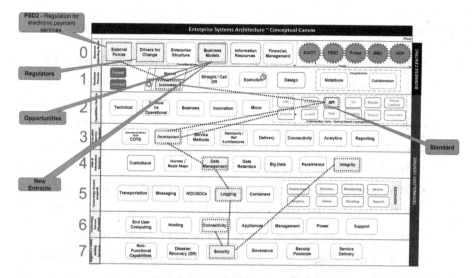

Figure A-4. *PSD-2 candidates that may be impacted for financial organizations*

The following table highlights some obvious candidates in the ilustration on our stack. They can form the basis for a level 0 architectural design.

Layer	Impact and Potential Areas for Initial Architectural Assessment
0	• The external force is the PSD-2 EU regulation. • The drivers for change are the regulation and the demands of the regulator. The business model provides new opportunities but also the threat of new tech-savvy entrants to the market.
1	• A major impact would be the automation of existing or new business processes to accommodate the workflow around the use of open APIs. This use of open APIs will require a deep understanding of the information that needs to be exchanged, i.e., the data schema and validation rules.

(*continued*)

Layer	Impact and Potential Areas for Initial Architectural Assessment
2	• The obvious impact is seen from or on the API ecosystem, the drive for standards, and how these standards will affect existing data exchange rules adopted by the organization. • Any impact on customer channels, e.g., websites/payment methods services and may require refactoring to accommodate the new change should be explored and a gap analysis performed. • Communication channels such as email for notifications may also need to be factored in as the volumes and frequency may require adjustments.
3	• Development effort and cost for the creation or extension of existing systems functionality for the support of the API ecosystem and the new processes should be analysed and provisioned for.
4	• Data management is fundamental with regard to both processing and retention of all transactional data. • Integrity is an important variable for all transactions during the data life cycle.
5	• Logging will not only apply to transactional audit but also to session information (source/destination/duration/device/info, etc.).
6	• Connectivity between endpoints will require attention, and possible whitelisting between sites may need consideration.
7	As this is a major operating model transformation, it would be prudent to consider all elements at this layer with an emphasis on security.

The previous table represents a cursory view of some initial thoughts around possible change candidates in the technology ecosystem resulting from the possible changes in the BOM. However, this is presented for illustration purposes only and can be easily modified and expanded, if so desired.

Regulatory Change and Impact on the Stack: GDPR Example

In May 2018 the European Union's General Data Protection Regulation (GDPR) [21] came into force, representing the regulation for data protection, privacy, and the transfer of personal data outside of the EU and the European Economic Area (EEA).

The GDPR had a major impact on the way the organization collected, processed, transformed, stored, presented, and consumed information. This impact prior to the law coming into force required organizations to analyze the subsequent impact on their technology landscape and any new capabilities to ensure compliance.

By mapping any regulatory specific items to the impacted areas of the stack will provid, a cursory view of the initial areas to ensure compliance from the technology estate.

Figure A-5 highlights the impacted areas that will require effort and adjustment and in many cases recalibration of existing legacy systems to meet the new legislative requirements.

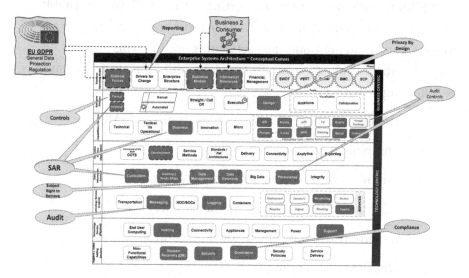

Figure A-5. *Mapping the impact of the GDPR onto the stack*

Each impacted area is discussed briefly in the following sections.

Business Operating Model

The key driver for change from the regulation was the potential fines for noncompliance, which influenced changes to the BOM.

The appointment or nomination of an organization data protection officer (DPO), while a standard function in many government agencies and departments, is now replicated in the nongovernment sectors.

Consideration needs to be given to methods and techniques for presenting, pulling, consuming, and pushing information in and out of the organization.

Business Processes

Many organizations modified their BOM and core business processes, with a major impact on existing projects that needed be recalibrated to meet the requirements of the GDPR.

Additional management and reporting of the GDPR was inevitable, and organizations reevaluated existing business and technical process (triggers, execution methods, data sets) for reporting. This analysis resulted in the introduction or refinement of additional processes such as the following:

- The management of subject access requests (SARs)

- Complaints receipt and handling

- Notifications (received and sent) to data subjects

- Information retention (audit/traceability)

- Governance of data and associated controls

- The DPO in their duties

Capabilities Services

The channels of data exchange between the enterprise and data subjects required review and in many cases updating, as this is the point at which the subject provided their data to the enterprise.

Organizations in some cases would be required to develop new systems and extend business capabilities and in many cases provision new services that support internal and external information exchange requirements.

Examples of impacted or potential new services are as follows:

- Services that facilitate privacy as a macro or micro service by default

- Possible notification services (SARs, etc.)

- Extension of reporting services

- Revaluation of channels for information dissemination such as pervasive devices, web portals, etc.

Applications

Applications that interacted with users and captured information required evaluation to ensure that consent was freely given for the use of this information.

In the case of commercial off-the-shelf packages, the requirement could easily be pushed back to the vendor/supplier. However, custom development may have required refactoring.

Applications that extract, transform, and push or pull subject data to any third-party system internal or external to the organization would require analysis and, in many cases, were flagged for recalibration to ensure they remained compliant with the GDPR.

Data and Information

GDPR is a data-centric policy and therefore impacted the way information was collected, transformed, shared, and persisted both internally and externally to the organization.

Analysis of existing stores and custodians of the stores required analysis, especially as full transparency must be shown for who has access rights to the data and how those access rights were controlled.

DPOs required new reporting data stores to enable them to perform their duties in terms of analysis and regulatory reporting where any data transferred outside of the organization and outside of the country of operation required closer scrutiny.

Data and information insights had to be developed to ensure compliance was not only met but also shown to be met down to data objects in physical databases.

Technology Services

Most technology services, i.e., the enablers, require semi-analysis as there may be a need to analyze how the information flows are orchestrated, both in and out of these domains. Examples are as follows:

- *Messaging systems*: Endpoints will require analysis.

- *Logging systems*: These will need to be analyzed to see if user information is persisted, and if not, anonymized, and then how the information is used.

- *Enterprise service bus*: If an enterprise service bus (ESB) is used, how, if any, is user data transformed during its journey through the bus and attached systems.

- *Reporting engines*: How are these leveraged, and can they be reused?

Hygiene Services

The following are hygiene services:

- *Disaster recover system*

  Most organizations have disaster recovery (DR) capabilities, which can be placed on standby (hot or cold). These standby systems hold information that requires synchronization at frequent intervals to ensure that if a system crashed, they can be recovered to the specific point and within a specified time.

  These systems are designed to retain data; however, where these systems are not a true replica of live production enviornments, then they may require additional analysis in terms of the retention of user data.

- *Security*

  One of the requirements of the GDPR is the production of data protection impact assessments (DPIAs). One can argue that UK government security officers produce similar information in the form of risk management and accreditation document set (RMADS) for secure accredited systems.

  RMADS for government functions may encapsulate much of what is required in the DPIAs. If applied to the government sector, a similar set of documents will need to be adopted by security or information assurance functions in the commercial sector.

ICT Strategy Pattern: ING Group Example/ Exercise

All companies produce annual reports; they are a kind of "state of the nation" for the organization and usually targeted at regulators, investors, and stakeholders in the business.

These reports provide a valuable source of information for any analysis, providing information on current activities, financials, and the future.

To demonstrate the use of the pattern discussed in Part 4, we will use a publicly available set of documents (the 2018 annual reports). The ING Group provides sufficient information to current and future investors on its public-facing website. The ING Group is a Dutch multinational banking and financial services corporation headquartered in Amsterdam. ING's primary businesses are retail banking, direct banking, commercial banking, investment banking, asset management, and insurance services.

Disclaimer   No discussion with any representative of the ING Group or associated companies or partners was undertaken, and all documentation is sourced from its public website for illustration purposes only: `https://www.ing.com` [22]. The section "Report of the Executive Board" provides enough information to demonstrate the steps to produce an ICT strategy for an organization.

STEP 1

A quick scan of the section "Our strategy and how we create value" highlights the priorities of the ING Group and provides adequate details on their business strategy. Step 1 is locate and extract keywords. Figure A-6 illustrates this at a macro level.

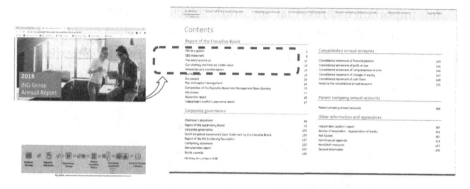

Figure A-6. *Sample business strategy (source: ING.COM)*

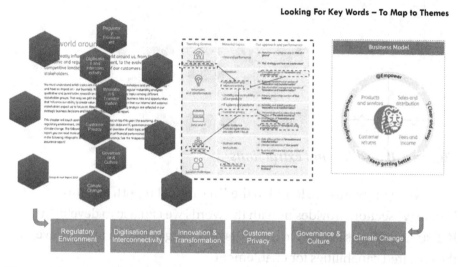

Figure A-7. *Locating keywords*

Locating the keywords is not an exact science and requires several attempts. Keywords often may not be obvious on the first pass but at a minimum should highlight areas of focus. In ING's case, our first scan shows a range of keywords from regulatory environments to climate change.

It is important to stress that any words selected from a third-party set of documents will be subjective. The opposite applies when working in the organization; one would have inside knowledge of the organizational priorities.

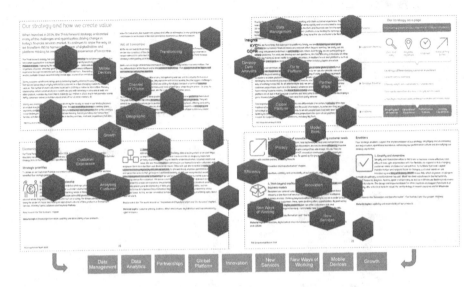

Figure A-8. *Additional extractions*

Several keywords are found in the ING annual report, and the "Strategy" section provides us with the words we can use to develop a full ICT strategy that is aligned to the goals of the organization and to develop the required capabilities for enablement.

Figure A-9 shows all the words we have extracted from the annual report; context can be gathered with further analysis if required. However, this now provides input to the next step, i.e., extraction of technology themes.

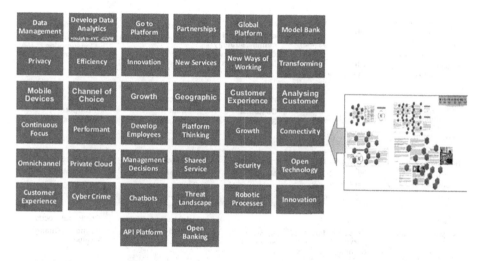

Figure A-9. *Default words extracted from ING annual report's "Strategy" section*

STEP 2

In step 2 we take the keywords extracted and map them onto technology themes and the system capabilities required to service the business strategy.

Keywords may reflect capabilities in some cases but allow us to expand and add additional context/information. For example, data management in our example is expanded to encapsulate the collection, extraction, transformation, and loading of single-view techniques, and we extend data analytics to infer the adoption of big data principles. This expansion work should be performed by the architect or subject-matter expertise for the domain.

Figure A-10. *Derived technology themes*

Figure A-10 summarizes the technology themes used to develop the system capability matrix, i.e., the top-level registry of all services provided to support the business.

Further analysis, e.g., an audit of the existing technology capabilities, should go hand in hand with this top-down approach, thus enabling the details to show gaps in the services offered to the business.

Figure A-11 highlights the capabilities and introduces the technology elements either from the audit of the estate or from other sources of information e.g., the CMDB.

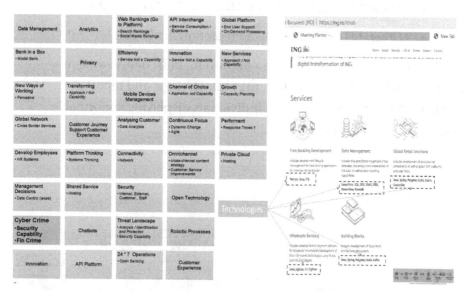

Figure A-11. *Extrapolating technology capabilities*

Each capability will require a deep dive by domain experts to define any gaps and provision costs for the remediation work proposed.

A good example in our example is the cybercrime capability, which is quite a wide topic, but we focus on two areas, general security capabilities and financial crime, that ING, being a financial institution, is subject to across all its markets.

As the ING Group is headquartered in Europe and operates in the United Kingdom, here are examples of the acts of parliament (UK) and EU regulations that are applicable and must be accommodated:

- *Anti-money laundering (AML)*: Sanctions and Anti-Money Laundering Act 2018

- *Fraud*: The Fraud Act 2006

- *Bribery*: The Bribery Act 2010

- *Terrorism*: The Financial Anti-Terrorism Act 2001

- *Market Abuse*: Regulation (UK FCA/ EU No 596/2014)

- *Other*: EU GDPR, UK Data Protection Act 2018

To remain compliant, ING, at a minimum, must deliver system capabilities that allow it to detect, prevent, manage, and report on noncompliant transactions or on individuals displaying abnormal transitional patterns behaviors.

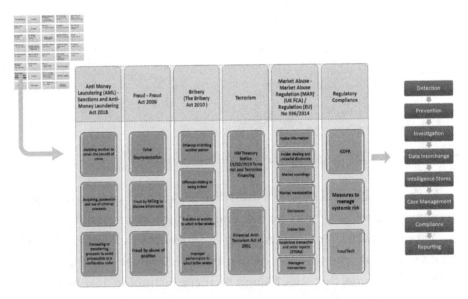

Figure A-12. *Financial crime example for domain/capabilities mapping*

Figure A-12 illustrates how a high-level capability called "Cybercrime" can be further decomposed when considering mandatory compliance areas. Exploring the inventory of existing systems will expose gaps in capabilities, especially where the following services are required:

- *Detection*: The ability to detect noncompliant transactions or individuals across its entire business portfolio

- *Prevention*: The ability to detect patterns of noncompliant behavior and transactional integrity to trigger alerts to invoke adequate responses

- *Investigation*: The tools to support the investigation of criminal behavior both by customers and by internal staff

- *Data interchange:* The ability to securely exchange information between various systems and third-party systems

- *Intelligence stores*: The ability to securely store information relating to criminal behavior or possible threats to ING

- *Case management*: The ability to manage a criminal case from alerting to court case

- *Compliance*: Systems to support the regulatory compliance.

- *Reporting*: The ability to generate reports on any of the previous activity

The previous highlights the level of decomposition required to derive the systems capability matrix, which requires analysis of both the required business capabilities and the inventory of existing systems.

STEP 3

In step 2 we highlighted the need to decompose high-level capabilities further to create the technology service inventory. During this process high-level costs will emerge to either fill the gap or remediate any shortcomings.

To manage and prioritize the costs associated with the maintain, adopt, adapt, shape variables for any investment portfolio for the organization, it would be prudent to segment the spend into the following categories:

- *Existinge* is unavoidable and is provisioned to support the existing levels of service and in essence "keep the lights on." This is often referred to as a *business as usual* (BAU) expenditure and easily estimated as it is derived from historic cost figures with a percentage for contingency spend.

  The goal with regard to this type of expenditure is to reduce it where possible or to keep it constant but not increase.

  It should be noted that any capital-type expenditures to acquire, upgrade, and maintain physical assets such technology or equipment be factored in as part of the technical debt provision.

- *Regulatory spend* is expenditure that is required to statutory obligations and is unavoidable. A recent example can be found in the recent move by insurance companies to adopt the Global Insurance Industry accounting standard IFRS 17 [23] where the spend is necessary to meet future industry compliance requirements.

- *Innovation or disruptive* expenditure is set aside to accommodate areas that cannot be easily quantified but can add value to the organization to disrupt the market and provide a competitive advantage or simply provide efficiency gains to operations.

- *Strategic* spend is the provision for an expenditure to meet and deliver the new capabilities identified during the analysis of the business strategy.

  A possible example of this may be experimentation cost. In the case of a finance organization, this may be the concept of an open banking platform exposing the platform to third parties and allowing them to leverage core banking services.

STEP 4

The final step outlined in the strategy pattern is the realization element, i.e., deploying systems of the strategy such as the component required to deliver the capabilities.

This step is a triad of services.

- *Control* refers to the mechanisms to successfully deliver the programs/projects to deliver the capabilities.

- *Execute* refers to the run of the capabilities.

- *Monitor* refers to the monitoring of the service to maintain service levels and remediate any possible problems that may arise.

This step is not an architectural service but one in which the architect will provide input to fine-tune the step.

In the previous exercise, we illustrated a path from a business strategy to an ICT strategy.

1. The target operating model/business strategy (corporate/functional) provides the drivers for the technology strategy.

2. Technology themes allow the business to have traceability between the ICT and the goals of the organization.

3. Dissect the themes to map to future, current, and innovation capabilities that drive the agenda of the business forward at the least unit of cost.

4. Split these capabilities into buckets (step 3) to allow the ICT budgets to be assigned and managed further.

5. Execution is the enabler for the business to continue functioning (step 4).

With this in mind, we have demonstrated a method to construct elements for an ICT strategy. As an exercise, you may want to select a similar type of organization and repeat the steps.

Example Table of Contents for an ICT Strategy

The hardest part of writing an ICT Strategy is 'putting pen to paper' which is never easy, despite having done all the preparatory work. Here we suggest a simple structure you may wish to adopt as a framework to create and deliver the ICT Strategy Document. The structure should be modified, to meet the any audience needs, but in providing we offer a starting point. Here is an example of an ICT strategy:

- *Document controls*
  - Strategic objectives
  - Background
  - Purpose of document
  - Intended audience
  - Intended usage and lifecycle
  - Related documents

- *Management Summary*
  - Summary of the Document Contents/Context

- *Part 1, Business Drivers: Business-Centric Content, Context*
  - Assessment, strategic/operational
  - Cost proposals (OpEx/Capex)
  - Initiatives
  - Value streams
  - Aligning the business strategy to IT outcomes
  - Business themes
  - Transposing the business themes into technology themes
    - Automate
    - Innovate
    - Collaborate
    - Optimize, kill complexity
  - Architecture principles
  - Governance
    - Business
    - IT
  - Policy and approach

- *Part 2: Technology Strategy: Technology elements*
  - Current technology ecosystem
  - Shadow IT
  - Known issues
  - Drivers for technology transformation and change
  - Cost breakdowns
  - Suppliers/vendors
  - Target model, reference architecture canvas
  - Capabilities definitions
  - Channels
  - API/data interchange
  - Process automation/robotics
  - Compliance/reporting information
  - Capability assessment and issues
  - Target end-state architecture
  - Proposed global standards
  - Roadmap and migration scenario(s)
  - Transition architectures
  - Appendix
    - Systems inventory by domain
    - Maturity levels guide
    - Acronym

Nonfunctional Requirements

Below are the some nonfunctional requirements you may wish to adopt and adapt towards your work for functional requirements gathering:

NFR	Comments/Attributes to Consider
Security (defining the key security requirements)	• Login/access levels for systems and individuals. • Create, read, update, and delete (CRUD) levels. • Access permissions for application data may be changed only by the system's data administrator. • Password requirements: Length, special characters, expiry, recycling policies, two-factor authentication (2FA). • Inactivity timeouts: Durations, actions, traceability. • System data backed up every x hours and copy stored in a secure offsite location. • Encryption (data in flight and at rest): All external communications between the system's data server and clients must be encrypted. Data classification/system accreditation: Should all data be protectively marked and how should it be stored/protected? Cost of providing the security in relation to the risk; i.e., the organizational risk appetite.

(*continued*)

NFR	Comments/Attributes to Consider
Audit (define the level of traceability for transactions required)	• System must maintain full traceability of transactions. • Audited objects are defined. • Audited database fields; which data fields require audit info? • File characteristics, size before, size after, structure. • User and transactional time stamps, etc.
Capacity (provisioning for growth)	• Throughput: How many transactions at peak time does the system need to be able to handle? • Storage (memory/disk): Volume of data the system will page/persist at runtime to disk. • Year-on-year growth requirements (users, processing and storage). • E-channel/VPN growth projections.
Performance	• Response times: Application loading, browser refresh times, etc. • Processing times: Functions, calculations, imports, exports. • Query and reporting times: Initial loads and subsequent loads, ETL times. • Interoperability: Data exchange packet rates.

(*continued*)

NFR	Comments/Attributes to Consider
Availability (uptime)	• Hours of operation. • Holidays, maintenance times, etc. • Locations of operation: Where should it be available from, and what are the connection requirements?
Reliability	• The ability of a system to perform its required functions under stated conditions for a specific period. • Mean time between failures: What is the acceptable threshold for downtime? • Mean time to recovery: If broken, how much time is available to get the system back up again?
Recoverability (in the event of failure)	• Recovery process. • Recovery point objectives (RPO). • Recovery time objectives (RTO). • Backup frequencies: How often is the transaction data, configuration data, and code backed up?
Robustness	• The ability of the system to resist change without adapting its initial stable configuration: operational characteristics with growth. • Fault trapping (I/O), application hooks, SMNP: How to handle failures?

(continued)

NFR	Comments/Attributes to Consider
Integrity (consistency of events, values, methods, measures, expectations, and outcomes)	• Application integrity. • Data integrity: Referential integrity in database tables and interfaces. • Information integrity: During transformation.
Maintainability (the ease with which the system can be maintained)	• Conformance to enterprise architecture standards. • Conformance to technical design standards. • Conformance to coding standards. • Conformance to best practices.
Usability	• User standards (look/feel). • User interface (UI) standards. • Internationalization/localization requirements: Languages, spellings, keyboards, etc.
Documentation	• User eocumentation. • System documentation (production acceptance?). • Help? • Training material.

Example of Five Ps Clustering

Architectural Principles, Practices, Processes, Patterns and Portfolio management (The 5 P's) provide, the cornerstone of delivering an EA capability to an organization, presenting a simple arrangement of activities and artifacts which can be mapped to the CID services of the EA function. Below we list some core areas under this 5P classification system.

Principles (I)	Practices (D)	Process (D)	Patterns (C,I,D)	Portfolio (C,I,D)
Business • This criteria element relates to the promotion of enterprise wide principles around the domain of business processing, especially business process modelling and service design. **Application** • Principles relating to the design, build and deployment of applications **Information** • Principles linked with the production, cleansing and publishing of information **Data** • Principles associated with data design, usage, persistence etc. **Infrastructure** • Principles associated with selection, deployment, management of the infrastructure (data Centers, Servers storage, network etc) **Foundation Services.** • Foundation services relate to DR, Security, Incident management etc i.e. services that are core to all of the above	**Business Operations** • Here Enterprise Architects should be concerned with the practices associated with capturing, modelling and digitally executing the business operations. **Application Design** • I.e. delivery of designs of. Whilst, practices adopted may based on a specific methodology or approach, the real question ' how efficiently have we adopted the practices of the approach and are we meeting the business demands based on this adoption ?' **Application Build** • The maturity of the build of applications both internal and externally developed applications should encapsulate test of software unit, components etc prior to build **Governance** • Architectural Governance and the teeth i.e. power of associated with the various boards. **Service Delivery** • The maturity of the practices i.e. what actually happens during the deployment, management of systems on the technology landscape. **Support** • Whilst this is close to Service Delivery it must be noted that we should rank how effectively the EA team deliver the support of its artefacts	**Business** • The engagement of the Enterprise Architecture functions with the Business Process Modelling and Design functions and any alignment activities. **STP** • EA should facilitate a move towards Straight Through processing i.e. reducing the number of digital and manual process hand offs between processes. **Information** • The Information Architecture and the associated process to capture, manage and publish EA information. **Orchestration** • This relates to the processes associated with orchestrating business and technology services **Production Acceptance** • The maturity of the processes associated with deployment, management of systems accepted into the production environment. **Documentation** • The maturity of document production , publication and promotion by the Enterprise Architecture function **3rd Party Engagement** • How effectively does EA engage with 3rd parties to maximise the benefits to the organisation e.g. cost reductions, savings etc **Contribution to the Enterprise** • What is the general perception of EA processes e.g. Governance contributing real value to the organisation from system users to senior management?	**Publications** • Does the organisation have a patterns catalogue? How mature is the organising in publishing it patterns, do these publications adopt standards for syntax, notations etc **Promotion** • How are patterns promoted through the organisation, are they rendered via an intranet? Or are they in a document library somewhere? **Development** • How patterns are developed – are they text book extracts or are they developed with the various technical communities? **Usage** • Do the technical Communities use these patterns to provide efficiency gains to the organisation? **Application** • Application patterns are to be found publically available and thus should be exploited – do your organisational developers for example exploit published patterns when constructing applications. **Infrastructure** • As with Applications above – Do your Service delivery personal for example use standard patterns for system configurations deployed into production. **Security** • Security patterns are emerging as a key in distributed systems – are these in use ?, does the technical community know of the existence **Re-Use** • How often are patterns re-used if at all and do we as an organisation promote reuse.	**Services** • Most Organisations have their own definition of a Services the EAM measure assumes a service as a function that is well-defined, self-contained, and does not depend on the context or state of other services. A service can be either a business or technical object. **Application** • The portfolio of applications in an Organisation can be a mix of either bespoke or Commercial Off the Shelf (COTS) either way the life cycle should be managed in a single unified location. **Middleware** • Middleware could refer to Enterprise Service Buses, Messaging or even request brokers – these should be managed and in most cases the interfaces to these systems. **Storage** • Information and data object persistence should be monitored and managed, i.e. not be the physical devices e.g. the NAS or SANs etc. **Servers** • The portfolio management of the Physical Servers both in the production and test environments. **Other Infrastructure** • Maturity of the portfolio management of the Physical devices e.g. network Switches, laptops, etc. **Techniques** • The techniques adopted to create, capture and manage the information required to measure the level of maturity in the management of the 'artefact' portfolio.

Third-Party Websites

The following are the websites referenced in the book. All URLs are valid at the time of writing.

Ref	Context	URL
1	A Framework for Measuring ROI of Enterprise Architecture	`https://pdfs.semanticscholar.org/dbd6/5c 1ee60125238185aa5985a33370624d0eb7.pdf`
2	2018 Deloitte Insights Report	`https://www2.deloitte.com/us/en/ insights.html`
3	UK MODAF Views	`https://www.gov.uk/guidance/mod- architecture-framework#viewpoints-and- views` `https://www.nato.int/cps/en/natohq/ topics_157575.htm`
4	US DODAF	`https://dodcio.defense.gov/Library/DoD- Architecture-Framework/`
5	TOGAF® Framework	`https://www.opengroup.org/togaf`
6	Zachman Framework	`https://www.zachman.com/about-the- zachman-framework`
7	Federal Enterprise Architecture Framework (FEA)	`https://obamawhitehouse.archives.gov/ omb/e-gov/FEA`

(continued)

Ref	Context	URL
8	SWIFT Data Standards (BIC, IBAN, LEI)	https://www.swift.com/standards/data-standards https://www.niceideas.ch/roller2/badtrash/entry/dissecting-swift-message-types-involved
9	ACORD: Insurance Industry Meta Model	https://www.acord.org/standards-architecture/reference-architecture
10	MODAF Meta Model	https://assets.publishing.service.gov.uk/government/uploads/system/uploads/attachment_data/file/48836/20090310_modaf_meta_model_v1_0-U.pdf
11	Jakarta EE	https://jakarta.ee/
12	Microsoft .NET Website	https://dotnet.microsoft.com
13	the Agile Manifesto	https://www.agilealliance.org/agile101/the-agile-manifesto/
14	Enterprise Integration Patterns: Hohpe/Woolf	https://www.enterpriseintegrationpatterns.com/patterns/messaging/

(continued)

Ref	Context	URL
15	UK Office of National Statistics	`https://www.ons.gov.uk/economy/` `environmentalaccounts/articles/` `environmentaltaxes/2015-06-01`
16	UN Sanctions List	`https://www.un.org/securitycouncil/` `content/un-sc-consolidated-list`
17	COBIT	`https://www.isaca.org/resources/cobit`
18	SFIA Framework	`https://www.sfia-online.org/en`
19	Open Group Architectural Principles	`Open Group Architectural Principles:` `https://pubs.opengroup.org/architecture/` `togaf9-doc/arch/chap20.html`
20	Business Model Alchemist (BMC)	`http://www.businessmodelalchemist.com/` `tools`
21	The full EU GDPR Text	`https://eur-lex.europa.eu/eli/` `reg/2016/679/oj`
22	ING Annual Report	`https://www.ing.com/About-us/Annual-` `reporting-suite/Annual-Report/2018-` `Annual-Report.htm`
23	International Accounting Standards Board	`https://www.ifrs.org`
24	SAFe®	`https://www.scaledagileframework.com/`

Glossary of Terms/Acronyms

The following are some of terms and acronyms used throughout this book:

Acronym	Label	Description
ABC	Activity-Based Costing	An accounting costing method that identifies activities in an organization and assigns the cost of each activity to all products and services according to actual consumption by each.
API	Application Programming Interface	A set of shared definitions and protocols for building and integrating application software between systems.
B2B	Business-to-Business	Refers to business that is conducted between companies, rather than between a company and individual consumers.
BAM	Business Activity Monitoring	Software and processes that support monitoring of business activities, key performance indicators, business/operational exceptions, and business risks, as those activities are implemented systems.
BIA	Business Impact Assessment	Establishes the consequences of a disruption of a business function or process and subsequently consolidates information needed to develop a set of recovery strategies for the business.
BPEL	Business Process Execution Language	Commonly known as Business Process Execution Language (BPEL). An OASIS standard executable language for specifying actions within business processes with web services.

(continued)

Acronym	Label	Description
BPM	Business Process Management	A discipline in operations management in which people use various methods to discover, model, analyze, measure, improve, optimize, and automate business processes.
BPMN	Business Process Model & Notation	A standard for business process modeling that provides a graphical notation for specifying business processes in a business process diagram (BPD), based on a flowcharting technique similar to activity diagrams from the Unified Modeling Language (UML).
BPR	Business Process Re-engineering	The process of restructuring a company's organization and methods, especially to exploit the capabilities of computers.
BVA	Business Value-Adding	A step or change made to the product that is necessary for future or subsequent steps but is not noticed by the final customer.
CapEx	Capital expenditure	The money an organization spends to buy, maintain, or improve its fixed assets.
CMDB	Configuration Management Database	A database used to store information about hardware and software assets of the organization. This database also stores information regarding the relationships among the assets.

(continued)

Acronym	Label	Description
CMMI	Capability Maturity Model Integration	A process model that helps organizations quantify maturity to encourage productive, efficient behaviors that decrease risks in software, product, and service development, which is assigned one of the five levels of maturity with the goal for improvement to reach level 5.

Level 1 – Initial.
Level 2 – Managed.
Level 3 – Defined.
Level 4 – Quantitatively Managed.
Level 5 – Optimizing.

Acronym	Label	Description
CRM	Customer Relationship Management	A technology for managing all your company's relationships and interactions with customers and potential customers.
DES	Discrete-Event Simulation	The process of codifying the behavior of a complex system as an ordered sequence of well-defined events. In this context, an event comprises a specific change in the system's state at a specific point in time.
EA	Enterprise Architect	We use EA throughout this book; however, we are referring to the Enterprise Systems Architect (ESA) with a bias on the systems side of responsibilities.
ERP	Enterprise Resource Planning	Business process management software that allows an organization to use a system of integrated applications to manage the business and automate many back-office functions related to technology, services, and human resources.

(continued)

Acronym	Label	Description
ETL	Extract, Transform, and Load	Three core enterprise data management functions that when combined seek to pull data out of one or more data stores and place it into another data store.
FDD	Feature-Driven Development	An iterative and incremental Agile approach to software development that places priority on the backlog for client-valued functionalities and operations.
FOCUS	Frame, Organize, Collect, Understand, Synthesize	The acronym from Paul Friga from the McKinsey Engagement Model that represents the Team FOCUS Framework for problem solving.
KPI	Key Performance Indicator	A measurable value that demonstrates how effectively a company is achieving key business objectives.
KPI	Key Performance Indicator	A type of performance measurement to indicate the performance against a scale that is used to monitor a activity or system.
KRI	Key Risk Indicator	A measure or value placed against an activity or platform to indicate a level of risk associated with it. KRIs are metrics that provide an early signal of increasing risk exposures.
O2C	Order to Cash	Refers to a top-level business processes for receiving and fulfilling customer orders.
OpEx	Operational expenditure	An ongoing cost for running a platform or business.

(continued)

Acronym	Label	Description
PDCA	Plan-Do-Check-Act	Sometimes seen as Plan-Do-Check-Adjust (PDCA); a repetitive four-stage model for continuous improvement (CI) in business process management.
RFQ	Request For Quote	A document that an organization submits to one or more potential suppliers eliciting quotations for a product or service.
ROI	Return-On-Investment	Measures the gain or loss generated on an investment relative to the amount of money invested.
SCADA	Supervisory Control and Data Acquisition	A computer system for gathering and analyzing real-time data used to monitor and control a plant or equipment in industries.
SCOR	Supply Chain Operations Reference Model Smart	A management tool used to address, improve, and communicate supply chain management decisions within a company and with suppliers and customers of a company.
SDLC	Software Development Life Cycle	The process for planning, creating, testing, and deploying an information system encapsulating the full cradle to grave services.
SOA	Service-Oriented Architecture	A style of software design where services are provided to the other components by application components, through a communication protocol over a network.

(continued)

Acronym	Label	Description
TOC	Theory of Constraints	A management paradigm that views any manageable system as being limited in achieving more of its goals by a very small number of constraints.
TQM	Total Quality Management	A core definition of Total Quality Management (TQM) that describes a management approach to long-term success through customer satisfaction. In a TQM effort, all members of an organization participate in improving processes, products, services, and the culture in which they work.
UML	Universal Modeling Language	A standardized modeling language consisting of an integrated set of diagrams, developed to help system and software developers for specifying, visualizing, constructing, and documenting the artifacts of software systems, as well as for business modeling and other nonsoftware systems.

Bibliography: Suggested Further Reading

- *Koch, Richard (1998). The 80/20 Principle: The Secret of Achieving More with Less. New York: Doubleday. ISBN: 9780385491747.*

- J. L Pappas, E.F. Bringham, B. Shipley. *Managerial Economics.* ISBN: 0-03-910426-5.

- Michael E. Porter. *Competitive Advantage: Creating and Sustaining Superior Performance.* ISBN: 0-02-925090-0.

- Harvard Business Essentials. *Strategy: Create and Implement the Best Strategy for your Business.* Harvard Business Press. ISBN: 978-1-59139-632-1.

- Thomas Erl. *Service-Orientated Architecture Concepts, Technology and Design.* ISBN: 0-13-185858-0.

- Kenneth S. Rubin. *Essential SCRUM.* ISBN-10: 0137043295.

- Gregor Hohpe, Bobby Woolf. *Enterprise Integration Patterns – Designing, Building, and deploying messaging solutions.* ISBN: 0-321-20068-3.

- John Sherwood Andrew Clark, David Lynas. *Enterprise Security Architecture: A Business Driven Approach.* ISBN: 1-57820-31§8-x.

- Charles T. Betz. *Architecture Patterns for IT Service Management, Resource Planning, and Governance.* ISBN 10: 0-12-370593-2.

- Jeanne W. Ross, Peter Well, David C Robertson. *Enterprise Architecture as a Strategy: Creating a Foundation for Business Execution.* ISBN 10: 978-1-59139-839-4.

- Paul N. Friga. *The McKinsey Engagement.* ISBN: 978-0-07-149741-1.

- Ambroise Goikoetxea. *Enterprise Architectures & Digital Administration: Planning, Design and Assessment.* ISBN: 978 9812 700285.

Cheat Sheet: Architectural Impact Assessment

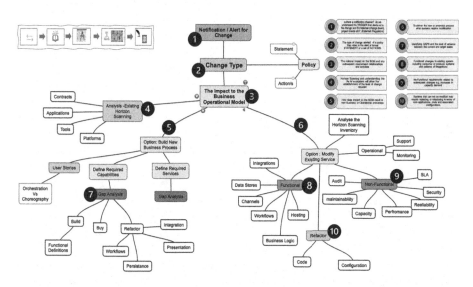

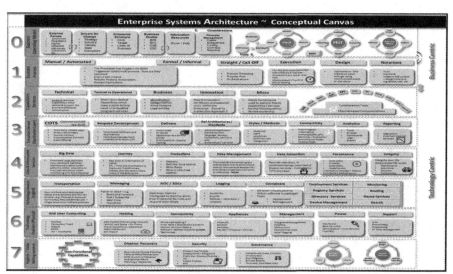

Index

A

Account information service
      provider (AISP), 241, 242
ACORD Reference
      Architecture, 21
Acquisition views (AcVs), 12
Agile approach, 145
Agile software development
      method, 94
All views (AVs), 12
Analytic and business intelligence
      (BI) applications, 97, 98
Appliances, 79, 127
Application as a service (AaaS)
      model, 84, 90
Application inventories, 83, 148
Application layer
   AaaS model, 84
   Agile Scrum flow, 94–97
   Agile software development
      method, 94
   alert reporting, 101
   analytics/business
      intelligence, 97, 98
   bespoke development, 91
   compliance reports, 101
   consideration summary, 102
   COTS, 89, 90

   dashboards, 101
   development practices/
      methodologies, 92
   in-house/out-source, 92
   inter-application
      connectivity, 98–100
   level 0 reference architecture, 86
   level 1 reference model, 88
   multiple internal services, 84
   operational reports, 101
   organizations, 83, 84
   reference architectures,
      85, 87, 88
   reporting applications, 100, 101
   Scrum, 94
   service, 84
   standards, 89
   waterfall, 93, 94
Application programming
      interfaces (APIs), 38, 76, 98,
      147, 185, 214, 239–241
Application reference models, 156
Applications, 83–102, 247
Archimate, 63, 153
Architects, 193
   enterprise architects,
      194–198, 208
   primary types, 194

© Daljit Roy Banger 2022
D. R. Banger, *Enterprise Systems Architecture*,
https://doi.org/10.1007/978-1-4842-8646-3

Printed in the United States
by Baker & Taylor Publisher Services